Afghanistan Through Passages of History

AFGHANISTAN THROUGH PASSAGES OF HISTORY

DR. SURAYIA GULL (NAQATI)

KANISHKA PUBLISHERS, DISTRIBUTORS
NEW DELHI-110 002

KANISHKA PUBLISHERS, DISTRIBUTORS
4697/5-21 A, Ansari Road, Daryaganj
New Delhi-110 002
Phones : 2327 0497, 2328 8285
Fax : 011-2328 8285
E-mail: kanishka_publishing@yahoo.co.in

First Published 2008

ISBN 978-81-7391-979-4

PRINTED IN INDIA

Published by Madan Sachdeva for Kanishka Publishers, Distributors, 4697/5-21A, Ansari Road, Daryaganj, New Delhi-110 002, Typeset by Sunshine Graphics, Delhi, and Printed at Nice Printing Press, Delhi.

Dedicated

to

My Grandfather

Gulam Mohammad Rafeeq

(1904–1995)

Founder of Alamdar-i-Kashmir

Research Foundation,

Sringar, Kashmir

Foreword

History of Afghanistan is of great antiquity and dates back to the pre-historic times. Despite difficult terrain and hazardous mountain passes, its significance in terms of modern concepts of geopolitics remained a prime issue. During the Ghandhara Civilization, Afghanistan was holding a pivotal position not less in significance when compared to the onward march of Alexander to the east.

The foot prints of the civilisational shifts and epochs are written large of the geographical contours of Afghanistan. The rugged mountain terrain of extreme climates and a stage of great games, had shaped to social fibre of its populace into well-knit clan system. Life or death when compared to the honour and dignity of the Afghan has no meaning. Their faith, in their religion is ultimate and in no case are ready to compromise. They are daring souls when they come to defend their honour, country and faith.

They have witnessed the onslaughts of the Britishers in 19th century, the Russian wrath in 20th century and the American missionaries of 21st century. The Afghans have learnt the lesson of an expert Shikari who fatigues his prey by forcing him to run, run and run till he loses his energy and finally preys upon him. The turban of an Afghan is his head gear, symbol of honour, a prayer carpet a blanket sheet of bed, a long cloth to carry his material things, and if dead serves the purpose of a shroud, so he has nothing to be afraid of. It is a strange phenomenon that life to an Afghan is just to pluck a flower from a Shrub, but when he gives asylum, even to his most dreaded enemy. He sacrifices himself but never allows any harm to prevail upon his asylum seeker.

Taking into consideration the aforesaid facts of the people and their country, for a researcher it becomes very difficult to understand the traits of the Afghan unless one devotes deep into the body physique of the people and the country.

The present attempt is additional to the literature already available on the people and the country. This book will give an idea to the students who are interested in the history and the culture of Afghanistan.

Prof. Abdul Majeed Mattoo
Ex-Director CCAS and Dean Faculty of Social Science, University of Kashmir, Srinagar (J & K)

Preface

Afghanistan, which for many reasons claims our particular attention is not only remarkable as being a link between the Indian and Middle Asiatic Nations, but also as having at different periods played as a conspicuous part in history. These Afghan people seem to appear first in the seventh century of the Christian era.

It is a well-known, fact that every history begins with fables and traditions. The commencement of history is either in age or the country in local situation, from those who attempt to preserve that history in records. A long time after a nation has fully formed itself is generally required before mere chroniclers become historians who knowhow to shift traditions from real facts and higher a degree of civilization a nation has obtained and more refined its task is, the less its historians allow themselves to indulge in relating traditions which are entirely banished from their works, or at least minutely discussed and divested of their embellishments and if possible reduced to their original facts. Such is the case in Ancient Romans and Greek authors as well as in those of our age and the first attempt that were made to write a history produced mere recorders abounding with tradition. It will appear at the first sight that the early history of Afghans rests on traditions which were repeated by every Oriental writer upon the subject and have even induced learned Europeans to attach credit to them.

The present work is an insight into geopolitical and historical perspective of Afghan territory along with periodicity in Afghan turmoils. The book figures out economic profile and defends Afghanistan as a nation state on the basis of its own historical and geographical perspectives.

Dr. Surayia Gull (Naqati)

Preface

Acknowledgements

"Allah alone is besought for help and on him alone we depend"

Complete acknowledgement of all that one owes to ones benefactors is an impossible task however, few words should be in order;

- Appreciations are due to all Colleagues of Centre of Central Asian Studies, University of Kashmir particularly to Prof. Gulshan Majeed, Prof. G.R.Jan, Prof. M.A Kaw, Dr. G.N. Khaki (Reader), Dr. Ajaz. A Banday (Reader), Dr. Raja Bano (Reader), Dr. A. Rauf Shah, Dr. Darakshan Abdullah, Dr. T. A Rather, Dr. Mohd Afzal Mir, Dr. Rafi-ud-din Makhdoomi, Dr. Tabasum Firdous, Dr. Afaq Aziz, Dr. Javid Talal and Dr. Mushtaq Ahmed Halwayee for their erudite and humanistic approach who helped me in various capacities while completing this work.

- Exceptional Gratitude to Prof. Ghulam Mohi-ud-din Mir, Director, Centre of Central Asian Studies for his valuable suggestions on various issues regarding the project particularly at the critical point of time of my understanding and knowledge are also due. His throughout concern has transcended all limits of academic zeal and enthusiasm for me.

- Thanks are also due to Professor Nisar Ali, Dean Faculty of Social Science for his precious suggestions and encouragements.

- As a matter of fact, this work is a result of sheer labour of so many well wishers and each one who has helped in any capacity i.e., verbally or providing relevant information or in any other capacity deserves sincere gratitude Prof. N.A.Nadeem, Head, Department of Education, University of Kashmir is prominent among them.

- I am equally indebted to my life-Partner Mr Gulzar Ahmad Naqati who stood like a rock throughout my academic pursuits.

- All appreciation to Friends, Scholars, Academicians, Well Wishers and Directorates of various Research Institutes, Libraries at New Delhi for extending their cordial support and co-operation during my stay at Delhi.

- My thanks, appreciations are also due to Ex V.C. Prof. Abdul Wahid Qurashi, & Ex-Registrar Prof. Mehraj-ud-din for their moral support.

- Last but not the least appreciation and thanks are also for our present Vice-Chancellor. Prof. Riyaz Ahmad Panjabi and Registrar Sayed Fayaz Ahmad Shah.

Dr. Surayia Gull (Naqati)

Contents

INTRODUCTION

PROFESSOR SHRI PRAKASH
Deputy Director
Academy of Third World Studies, Jamia Millia Islamia University, New Delhi.

Dr. Surayia Gull, a Research Associate at the Centre of Central Asian Studies, University of Kashmir, Srinagar has described and analyzed the complex history of Afghanistan from the second-half of the nineteenth century uptill the present times. The theme in itself is an important one because it concerns the anlysis of political and economic processes through which different tribes, the Pashtuns, Tajikas, Uzbeks and Hazaras speaking distinct languages but believing in Islam were brought together through the intervention of external forces – the British and the Russians in the nineteenth century; the Soviets and now in the post-Taliban phase an international group consisting of many countries – USA, Russia, India, China, Pakistan, Japan, the ECO nations to form a modern constitutional state consisting today of an elected government, independent judiciary, bureaucracy and a free media. The paradox of modern Afghan history is that despite the willingness of the tribes to come together in a Loya Jirga – a Grand Assembly of the representatives of the different tribes – to sanction the setting up of a modern state on several occasions the traditional authority of the tribal organizations at the local level his prevented both democratic and communist states from being effective as well as functional. It remains to be seen whether the present effort at building a modern nation state will lead to the development of a new economy based on modern educational system managed and run by a technocratic, skilled elite as well as a trained working class.

Despite the new constitutional architecture, the presence of the US Armed Forces to prevent the return of the Taliban who are still present and active in the southern and south western parts of

Afghanistan is a constant threat to the stability of the coalition government led by Hamid Karzai. It seems that a distinction has to be made between a Loya Jirga called together spontaneously and one convened by authorities supported or associated by external powers and forces. The latter kind does not command the instinctive loyalties of the local tribesmen and today in Afghanistan this is reflected in low revenues paid to the government and a lack of enthusiasm for working hard to revive the economy. A less than edequate domestic mobilization for building a modern nation state has made the present Afghan Government overtly and excessively dependant on external aid which again is seen by the so-called 'traditional forces' as foreign intervention in their internal affairs.

However, one has nonetheless to recognize that following the UN resolutions declaring the Taliban State as illegal and formed on the basis of force without the consent of the people, mandatory sanctions were imposed against the Taliban regime for its contemptuous violation of human rights especially those of women. The military intervention under UN aegis was also due to the fact that the Talibans were a militia and ruled virtually through arbitrary martial law and would not have given up power without being forced to do so. Even now the head of their organization Mullah Omar remains at large, hiding, it is suspected in the Pashtun region of Pakistan. Even otherwise several other regions of Afghanistan are not entirely under the control of the Central Government. Even normally the President Hamid Karzai moves around with heavy primarily American military escort and there have been some attempts on his life. That the Taliban who have now linked up with the Al-Qaida remain a force is attested to by the several attacks they have launched against US troops in Afghanistan. This shows how *instability* continues to be a major characteristic of the Afghan political system many years after the international intervention under UN leadership had ousted the illegal Taliban regime. It is this *instability* which the book analyzes and tries to answer the question whether lack of a social and political consensus or the difficult situation of the economy constitute the real explanation of the none too stable polity of present-day Afghanistan.

The Afghanistan Government's financial position is not healthy. The Budget Deficit in 2003-04 was 257.2 million US dollars. The people's condition is even worse. According to the World

Development Report of 2005 the average life expectancy at birth in 2002 was just 43 years the lowest anywhere and the under 5 mortality rate per 1000 was 257, the highest in the World.

Considering the disastrous situation which confronts Afghanistan today many international organizations and countries are making efforts to help in a variety of ways. The United Nations along with other international donors has sanctioned funds which would be used to make up a shortfall of 84,500 tons of cereal to help refugees and internally displaced people as well as people residing in remote areas. International donors are stepping up aid programmes to provide shelter for Afghan returnees. They expect to build 40,000 housing units to house around 3,00,000 Afghans by 2009. It is estimated that around 9,80,000 people are in dire need of shelter.

India is one of the important aid donors to Afghanistan showing that it makes no distinction between Muslim majority and other countries but favours consensual international efforts for promoting economic development, democratization and human resources growth. At the Jaunary 2002 Conference on "Reconstruction of Afghanistan" in Tokyo, India committed US dollar 100 million for rebuilding Afghanistan and later during one of President Hamid Karzai's many visits to India another 400 million. This money is meant for a wide range of developmental activities ranging from building schools, hospitals, roads, media, and providing training to judges, officials and security personnel. Hamid Karzai is himself a student of one of the Universities in India. India's aid to and trade with Afghanistan will increase rapidly once Pakistan gives free passage to India. Afghanistan has at the last 14th Summit of SAARC Heads of State held in New Delhi on 3rd and 4th April, 2007 officially joined the South Asian Association for Regional Cooperation as its 8th member. This has led to much greater international attention being paid to SAARC and Afghanistan's joining SAARC which was founded in 1985 was one of the factors which led many important organizations and countries China, Japan, South, Korea, USA and the European Union to attend the New Delhi SAARC Summit as observers for the first time. Iran too has applied to become on observer and is expected to attend the 15th SAARC heads of State Summit to be hosted by Maldives.

The International support for the reconstruction of Afghanistan is due to its crucial geopolitical position which makes it the shortest route connecting energy and mineral rich Central Asian Countries to Europe, West and South Asia. At present a pipeline connecting Turkmenistan with Pakistan for carrying gas supplies to Gwadhyr port located in Pakistan is being built. There are plans to connect existing road and rail networks built by the Soviet Union with China and Afghanistan. Afghanistan itself has large reserves of minerals and the potential for producing dry fruits, nuts and other food products apart from wool and related items.

The realization of Afghanistan's economic potential needs the building of a stable political system and further international aid. The International Red Cross Committee (ICRC) has launched a three to five years anti-parasite veterinary programme in order to tackle the diseases attacking Afghanistan's already decimated livestock. The programme concentrates on the provinces of Mazari-i-Sharif, Ghor and Bamian. The ICRC has treated around 50,00,000 animals in the last two years. Afghan farmers depend on animals for traction power during planting and harvesting as well as for fertilizer, fuel, milk, meat and wool.

Since March 2003 more than 1.5 million refugees have returned among when 3,00,000 are from Iran, 1.5 million from Pakistan and the rest are from Central Asia.

The Asian Development Bank has approved grants to repair the roads around Kandahar. It is also giving a four million US dollar grant to help rebuild the formal education system. About 750 teachers will get refresher training and about 1000 construction jobs will created. The grants for both these Projects have come from the Japan Fund for Poverty Reduction (JFPR) financed by the Japanese Government which has stepped up its involvement in Afghanistan. The Economic Cooperation Organization (ECO) which comprises Iran, Pakistan, Turkey, Afghanistan, Azerbaijan, Kazakhstan, Kyrgyzstan, Tajikistan, Turkmenistan and Uzbekistan has set-up another fund to help rebuild the war ravaged Afganistan. With so much of international support and activity to build a civil society as well as a modern economy and a democratic political system the forces like Taliban which want to reverse this process are at a disavantage. As Dr. Surayia Gull's book emphasizes, it needs greater cooperative effort and persistence to realize Afghanistan's historical destiny which has deluded it in the twentieth century.

1

Afghanistan: Geopolitical and Historical Perspective

Afghanistan,[1] which is a secluded and mountainous country with a backward economy, occupies a very important strategic and political position in southwest part of Asian continent. It is geographically, politically, historically, culturally and strategically a part of Central Asia connecting it with South Asia and the Middle East. Political and religious geography connect it with South Asia and Middle East. All these regions and beyond are directly affected by the happenings in Afghanistan. The recent events in the country, particularly since the rise of Taliban by capturing power in 1996, have reinforced the centrality and significance of Afghanistan, not only to the region but also to the world at large.

Geography

The total area of Afghanistan is 647,000 square kms. It is situated on the plateau that separates the countries of Central Asia from Pakistan. Afghanistan is situated to the north-west of Pakistan. It shares a land frontier with Pakistan to its south and east with Iran to its west and with Turkmenistan, Uzbekistan and Tajikistan to its north. It shares a 2,370 kms long border with the Central Asian Muslims Republics of Turkmenistan, Uzbekistan and Tajikistan in its north. The country also has a land frontier with the extreme northern part of India. The Wakhan Corridor in the north-east connects China with Afghanistan. This strategically important Corridor on the Pamirs brings Afghanistan in very close proximity with the strategic Karakoram Highway linking Pakistan with China. The river Oxus, now the Amu Darya, is Afghanistan's border with the former Soviet Union.

Afghanistan is the only country which communicates East Asia with West Asia, South Asia with Central Asia. Its spine running from north-east to south-west is the Hindukush, the flat lands to the north are part of Turkistan. Whole of this landlocked country is also called the land of Aryans. The early history of this area confirms that Indo-Aryan migrations from Central Asia across the Afghan mountains to the Indian subcontinent occurred about the middle of second millenniums BC. The Hindukush was a much dearer dividing line not only between Central and South Asia but also between yurt dwelling and black tent dwelling in the southwest and west of Iran. The Durand Line to the south separates it from Pakistan and forwards south east.

The boundaries of Afghanistan were established by Russians and the British. Great Britain and Russia agreed in 1873 AD that the river Oxus (Amu Darya) should be the northern frontier of Afghanistan. Afterwards in 1891 AD, Major General C. S. Maclean delineated the boundary between Persia (Iran) and Afghanistan. Two years later in 1893 AD, British Foreign Secretary, Mortimer Durand established the frontiers between British India and Afghanistan. The political boundaries between China and Afghanistan were also agreed between the Western imperial powers in 1895-96 AD. The Wakhan Corridor was forced upon Afghanistan in order to avoid direct contact between Russia and British India.

Historical Settings

Ahmad Shah Abdali established the state of Afghanistan in 1747 AD in the form of a tribal confederacy. However, the real founder of modern Afghanistan was Amir Abdur Rahman Khan (1880 AD-1901 AD). The most important changes in Afghanistan under Pashtun rule (since 1747 AD) occurred during the reign of Amir Abdur Rahman Khan. They include:

- The settlement of Pashtun in northern Afghanistan, regarded as Pashtun colonialism by the local, non-Pashtun peoples;
- The suppression of Hazara tribalism in Central Afghanistan, together with the granting of pasture rights to Pashtun nomads in this area; and
- Islamization of the Afghan society.

Pashtuns have always dominated the political and cultural life. Originally, this Pashtun rule stretched eastward as far as the River

Indus. However, in 1823 AD, the British Raj annexed 40,000 square miles of Pashtun dominated areas. The Durand Line formalized this partition in 1893 AD. Pakistan inherited this country in 1947, despite Afghanistan protests. Afghan claims over this territory land beyond, referred to as "Pakhtunistan, have been the main source of tension between Pakistan and Afghanistan.

The Great Game

The late 1800s witnessed the rivalry between two imperial powers: Great Britain and Russian. The Tsarist Russian expansion to the south was a direct threat to the security of India then governed by the imperial British government. Britain found Afghanistan and the Hindukush mountain ranges as natural boundaries and defence lines against Russian advance. The British considered the best way to checkmate Russian advance either by direct control of Afghanistan, or at least to make it inaccessible to the Russians. This partly explains the northward expansion of the Afghan state during the region of Amir Abdur Rahman Khan. The British actively sought to keep Afghanistan an inhospitable route to any advancing armies, particularly the Russians.[2] The Afghan rulers, including Amir Abdur Rahman Khan, considered the policy of keeping powerful neighbours at an arm's length. This policy may have helped in maintaining the country's independence, but it also kept the Afghan society out of reach for the benefits of modern educational, technological and socio-economic developments.

The dimensions of Afghanistan—from the Persian frontier at Kariz, on the Mashed-Herat road, to the borders of the British Indian Empire at the Khaibar Pass, the distance is approximately six hundred miles. The width of the country decreases as it runs from southwest to a point in the northeast, where an arm consisting of the narrow district of Wakhan, constitutes the eastern end of the Russo-Afghan boundary. At its broadest section, that represented by a line drawn on the Oxus to New Chaman, the distance would be some 450 miles. The total area aggregates 250,000 square miles, which is slightly larger than that of the territory of France.

Afghanistan may be described as the "Switzerland of South Asia." Both countries are essentially mountainous and contain main ranges and the sources of important rivers, both are situated inland, without any contact with ocean or sea. The other similarity these two countries have is that many different races or tribes inhabit both the countries.

The Boundaries

The limits of Afghanistan, until comparatively recently, were well-defined and, during the last fifty years have been settled by numerous commissions, which will be dealt with in this work.

Starting from Zulfikar Pass, at the north-west corner the boundary runs eastwards to Kushk, the terminus of a branch line of the Russian Central Asian Railways from the junction at Mercy. It follows a northeasterly direction and strikes the Oxus River in the Pamir, then forms the boundary of Afghan Turkistan, Badakhshan and Wakhan to Sir-i-Kul (Lake Victoria) on the Pamirs. The boundary continuing through the Lake follows the northern boundary of Wakhan to its junction with the Chinese Empire in the inaccessible range of Sarikol.

Turning south-westwards from this point, the frontier follows the crest of the Hindukush, bending gradually southwards and marching with the North West Frontier Province (NWFP) until it reaches Kafirstan. Here the lofty Shawal range running southwards divides the Bashgol further south Dir and Malakand lie on the British side of the frontier, and the Kabul-Peshawar frontiers is reached at Landi Kotal to the east of the historical Khaibar Pass and, passing below the Peiwar Kotal. It includes Waziristan on the Indian side of the boundary and reaches the borders of British Baluchistan at the Gomul Pass.

From Domandi, an uninhabited spot at the junction of the Kundar with the Gumal River, to Kush-i-Malik-i-Shah or "The Mountain of the Black Chief", were the frontiers of Persia reached, is a distance of over eight hundred miles. Generally speaking, it is a desert land with barren mountain ranges and vast open plains, possessing few inhabitants owing to lack of water and of security. Dry torrent beds with boulders or pebbles cover large areas, to be succeeded by equal large areas of sand dunes. The rare springs of water usually possess salt or unpleasant medicinal properties. But there are occasionally green wooded valleys with streams of pure water, fertile tracts which give immense pleasure to the travellers.

To give some details of this section, the boundary follows up the Kundar River to the highlands of Khuransan, rising to an altitude of 7,000 feet, where it divides the drainage flowing into Afghanistan to the north and west from that flowing into India in the south and east, the watershed is reached. The tribes on both sides of the frontier are Afghan, westwards there are Balochs and Brahuis. From Chagi, situated on the Lora Hamun, is the Registan Desert. Upon approaching the boundary of Persia, the Kuh-i-Taftan, rising to 12,600 feet, it is clearly visible.

The Guad-i-Zirra, which falls entirely to Afghanistan, is a salt water lake some twenty-five miles long, five miles wide and is occasionally fed, in years of exceptional flood, by overflow of water from the Helmand. From the mountain boundary of the three states, the Persian-Afghan boundary turns northeast to Kuhak, the site of a dam in the Helmand. Owing to the wayward nature of this river, British Commission settled the exact borderline and part of the Hamun was awarded to Afghanistan in 1903. Northwards, the boundary has quite recently been fixed throughout and strides the Hari Rud at a point where that river forms the boundary, at first with Persia and later with Russia.

Mountains

The Hindukush is the most important mountain range in Afghanitan. Ibn Battuta, the great Moslem traveller, wrote in 1334 AD, "The mountain is called Hindukush, since slave boys and girls who are brought from India die there in large number as a result of the extreme cold." The phalanx of Alexander the Great, termed it as the India Caucasus (it was the Paropanisus of Ptolemy). To quote Burrard. "This broad range has become divided by river into two parallel ranges both of which are long and important features" Farther west there is the lofty Kuhi-Baba. In Herat, it was incorrectly termed the Paropanisus by the nineteenth century European travellers.

The most important range on the eastern frontier is termed Safid Kuh with Sikaram reaching an altitude of 15,620 feet to the south of Jalalabad. There are some higher peaks in Kafirstan. On the eastern side there is a sudden descent into the Indus Valley. Consequently, with the exception of the plains of Afghan Turkistan, the whole country belongs to the Iranian plateau, which was itself a late geological formation of the tertiary period with its limestone and sandstone ranges. The central Afghanistan is occupied by numerous subsidiary ranges running parallel to the main range. These spurs extend southwest to Kandahar, while one, exceptionally long, forms the steep Khojak range which has been tunneled to allow the railway line from India to reach the Afghan frontier New Chaman.

The Strategic Question

From one point of view, Afghanistan may be considered as a mountainous region separating the civilization of the Euphrates from those of the Indus and the Oxus. Again, it can also be regarded as a region of caravan routes joining Central Asia to the plains of India, with cities such as Kabul, Herat and Kandahar.

Rivers

Few regions can claim our interest more strongly than the Pamirs. Aptly named Bamm-ud-Dunia or "Roof of the World", the Pamirs, lie at an elevation of some 13,000 feet uniformly shelving downwards from mountains covered with perennial snow, and constitute some great rivers of Asia. The Oxus flows westwards towards the Caspian Sea, the Yarkand River flows eastwards to the Gobi desert, while the Syr Daria and the Indus also take their origin from the Pamirs. Ptolemy had recognized its importance and called it *Mons Imaus*.

On the Afghan side of the pass at an elevation of 14,700 feet, the historical Oxus has its main source in a great glacier, to which small glaciers contribute. The Ab-i-Panja, flow in a westerly direction and at Kala Panja receives the Pamir River, flowing down from Sir-i-Kul (Lake Victoria). Seventy miles below Kala Panja, at a point near Ishkashim, the river makes its great northern bend round the states of Sihgnan and Roshan, which remained under Afghan possessions until they surrendered to Russia at the end of the nineteenth century.

While flowing in this northerly direction, the important Murghab or Aksu River (which crosses at the Russian headquarters of Pamirshi Post), increase the volume of the Oxus that still retains locally the name of Ab-i-Panja. The river concludes its great bend round the province of Badakhshan, and while flowing westwards, it receives the Wakshab on the right bank, and the frontier of Afghanistan until, in the neighbourhood of Kilif, where it is known as Amu Darya or Oxus. It turns to the north-west and finally joins the Aral Sea. The Oxus River, which is indeed the historical river of

Central Asia, is compared with the Rhine River of Europe. Other important rivers of Afghanistan are the Helmand, the Kabul and the Hari Rud. Some minor rivers, which provide water to the districts of Andkhui, Balkh and Kunduz, belong to the the Oxus basin.

The Helmand, also known as the classical Eytmander, which drains an area of 100,000 square miles, originates from the Hindukush between Kabul and Bamian at a considerable altitude, and traversing the Hazarajat, is joined at some thirty miles below Girishk by its most important tributary, the Arghandab. In its lower reaches, it flows through a cliff-sided trough a mile or two wide with villages at interval. The presence of Ammu ruins marks what was the ancient highway traversed by Alexander the Great, and it finally discharges into the Seistan, at an elevation of 1,600 feet.

The Kabul River, draining an area of 35,000 square miles, rises some 40 miles west of the Kabul city. Its chief tributaries are the Panjshir and the Kunar. It flows generally in an easterly direction towards Dakka and joins the Indus at Attock. Finally, the Hari Rud rises on the slopes of the Kuh-i-Baba and flows through extremely rugged country due west to the fertile valley of Herat. It turns to north near the Iranian frontier village of Kariz.

The Provinces

The city of Kabul situated at an altitude of 5, 850 feet with a population of 80, 000 is the Sanscrit Kubha and the Kophen of Arrian. The Kubha was one of the seven names of the valley. However, there is no mention of any ancient town that can be identified with Kabul.

Coming down the ages to the journey of the Chinese pilgrim Hieun Tsang, in the middle of the seventh century AD, the Chinese called Kabul as Kao-Fu. In 1504 AD, Babur captured Kabul and thereby laid the foundation of the Moghul Empire. He was impressed by the climate, the running streams, flora and fauna of the valley. Since the Great Game, Kabul had developed rapidly. A modern city with stately buildings sprung up, while palaces surrounded by gardens were erected by Abdur Rahman and his successors.

Writers in the past have considered Kandahar to be named after Alexander the Great. However, it is now established that the word "Kandahar" is a corruption of the ancient Indian state of Gandhara. Like Kabul, it was relatively unimportant until the middle of the twelfth century. It became part of the Moghul Empire although, as the Safavi Shahs of Persia constantly fought for possession of this city en route to Sindh. Shah was buried in it. Situated at an altitude of 3,340 feet, it possesses a population of 60,000 inhabitants. The Herat province owes its importance alike to its position and its fertility. Situated on the Hari Rud, both in appearance and population, it closely resembled the neighbouring Khurasan.

Situated at 3,030 feet, Herat was undoubtedly a premier centre of art and learning, comparable to that of the Italian cities of the Renaissance period. Herat was, generally speaking, a province of the Persian Empire under the Safavis, but was included in the kingdom of Afghanistan by its founder Ahmad Shah. This city with a population of some 30,000 inhabitants has become an important trade centre today. Caravans carrying hides, wool, dried fruits, pistachios and walnuts ply to the railhead at Kushuk. There is also a certain amount of trade with neighbouring Khurasan.

The Siah-Push or "Wearers of Black Clothes" were first recognised by Sir William Lockhart in 1885 AD. Holdich, who conducted the boundary survey in Afghanistan, describes them as "wild-looking men of Aryan features, with prominent noses, straight eyes, wide but expressive mounts." He adds, "their favourite pastime of racing down hill, where there is an occasional drop from terrace to terrace of ten to fifteen feet, on one leg."

The Kafirs were believed to be pagans. Their beliefs mingled with animism, but they worshipped many Gods, the chief of whom was Imra, the Creator. The Kafirs were converted to Islam by Amir Abdul Rahman, who renamed the country Nuristan or "Abode of Light." Progressed northwards they realize that India was protected by gigantic mountain barriers. The northeast, consisting of densely wooded mountain ranges with deep lateral valleys, constituted an impenetrable barrier against invading armies, while farther north the barren, frozen plateau of Tibet constituted an equally impregnable defence, as did the lofty mountains of Kashmir. It was only on the extreme of natural defence to India. Here in north of Chitral, commences the famous northwest frontier of India, and its land gates are situated.

The inhabitants of Afghanistan include Afghans, Persians and Turks (including the Uzbeks of the Oxus Valley, Mongols and Aryans of the Hindukush). Considerable inter-mixture has taken place yet each race has outstanding features. The Afghan nomads were organized through a tribal system, whose true national name is Pashtun or Pakhtun, generally termed "Pathan" by Europeans. They belonged to the Turko-Iranian type, with an admixture of Indian blood among the tribes bordering on the India's frontiers.

The *Hudud-al-Ala I*, which was compiled in 982 AD, reads, "Saul, a pleasant village on a mountain. In it, live Afghans," In this work, we also read that the King Ninhar (Ningrahar) had many wives. The first mention of the name Afghan is about thirty-years earlier than that given by *Hudud-al-Alam*. There was an earlier mention of Afghans by Masudi in his work *al-Tanbih*, completed in 956 AD. It states that "the *rubat* or fortified caravanserai of Badakhshan stands over various kinds of 'Turks' viz. only by a dot from Afghan.

The details about Afghans were also found in the *Tarikh-i-Yamini* of al-Otbi, Secretary of Mahmud of the Ghazni, as having been enlisted in the army of Sabuktigin and also of Mahmud himself. During this period, their habitat was in the Sulaiman mountains to the east of Ghazni. Its range culminates in the *Takht-i-Sulimand* or "Throne of Solomon." In this work, reference will be made to the grazing areas of various tribes and details of migrations made either by conquering tribes or by orders of the their rulers. It can be added that the Afghans are fanatical Muslims of the Sunni sect.

The sedentary Tajik population, whom the Afghans call nomads and the Persian element, the oldest established inhabitants of the country. The Tajiks, are village dwellers, as are their kin men in Persia (modern day Iran) and Central Asia. They probably occupied all the fertile areas of the country before the Afghans from the eastern mountains moved westwards. Organized in village communities, as in the neighbouring Persia, they formed a part until the middle or the eighteenth century, and supplied the traders and artisans of the towns.

The kingdom of Ghur, which overthrew the dynasty of Ghazni, was a Tajik dynasty, as was also the Kurt dynasty. Although, the Tajiks did not possess the outstanding material qualities of the Afghan tribesmen, they were courageous. The Tajiks adopted the tenets of Sunni Islam.

The Turks of Afghanistan, mainly the Uzbeks, occupy Afghan Turkistan where in the last century, they formed semi-independent Khanates. These Uzbeks of Afghanistan are closely related to their cousins in Central Asia, where Bukhara was a powerful Uzbek State.

The Hazaras

South of the Hindkush, in the mountains between Bamian and the Herat Valley, the inhabitants are of a distinctly Mongol type. Their ancestors are believed to have occupied this area after the devastations caused by Chenghiz Khan's attacks. The Hazaras were industrious cultivators. They were members of the Shia sect and were consequently despised and oppressed by the fanatics. Many of them used to enlist in high profile regiments of the British Indian army.

Islam and Resistance in Afghanistan

The spontaneous uprisings against the community regime which broke out in 1978 and 1979 were directed as much against the state itself as against the Communist government. The imposition of communism on the country may be seen as a new and even more radical phase with the penetration of the state bureaucracy in the countryside. These two dimensions, opposition to the state and the rejection of communism, are closely interlinked. Yet the attitude of the countryside towards the state has always been more ambivalent: the Afghan state was born in the tribal lands; the symbol of authority which it exercises is not alien to the peasant experience and many of the leaders of the resistance movements visualized a state for them - an Islamic state. At the same time, the recent history of Afghanistan is one of the revolts against the central authority and resistance to the penetration of the state bureaucracy in the countryside.

Contradiction between state and society is always somewhat artificial. Yet in Afghanistan, this separation is rooted in day-to-day experience. It is apparent in rural villages, where the administrative buildings are set apart from the people's dwellings. It may be seen in the clothes worn and the general behaviour of the individuals in society. For the peasants, the state is alien, and the relationship between the peasantry and the state officials is characterized by profound and mutual contempt. In fact, there is only one real town, Kabul, the capital, where, of course, the distinction between state and society is blurred. But there are really two Afghanistans: first there is the town (*Shahr*), the place of innovation (*Bidat*). This is the natural environment of the civil servants, teachers, soldiers and the communists, all "intellectuals" and "bare-heads" (*Sarluchad*), held to be unbelievers and arrogant. Secondly, there is the province (*Atraf*), the home of religion, tradition (*Sunnat*) and values which stand the test of time.

The game of politics is played out against each of these two backdrops. In the town, politics is followed attentively by students and the middle classes, whose very existence is bound up with the state, whereas it holds little interest for the peasants who only get news of what is happening in the town when he fiddles with the knobs of his radio in search of music. The "double-dealing of kings" (*Padshahgardi*) only affects him when it threatens to disturb the pattern of his daily life in some way. In the countryside, the drama of politics revolves around the struggle for local pre-eminence carried on by the Khans. They strive to enlarge their patronage, to be deferred to as judges in local disputes and thus increase their wealth and extend their family connections. In tribal zones, this struggle is sometimes violent, but it is carried on behind closed doors; whatever the outcome, it never has any effect on the traditional social structure.

There is constant interaction between these two social worlds, the form it usually takes is the gradual wearing away of rural society by the growth of state institutions and the tapping of state resources for the private use of groups within the community. Or it may take the more turbulent form of the cultural revolution instigated from above, as was the case with King Amanullah from 1924 to 1928, and under the Khalq regime in 1978 and 1979), accompanied by a general uprising in the countryside in the name of *Jihad* (as in 1928 and 1979). At such crucial junctures, ideological divisions transcend the narrower village and tribal groupings, which nevertheless make themselves felt in the forms of political organization (including that of the Communist Party).

What distinguishes the two camps--neither of which can be described as stable or homogeneous-cannot really be defined in sociological terms; it is their relation to the realm of politics that counts. The stereotype which equates the town with progress and the countryside with tradition has little basis in reality. In both town and country, there is a core of continuity. Urban society has changed a great deal since the time when it consisted almost entirely of a royal court and a bazaar; now, besides the aristocracy, there is a new state bourgeoisie of officials, students and soldiers whose very existence depends on the institutions they started. It must be added that real power wielders within these, which have been important since the thirties, comprise those who make their groups, whose identity is not clearly defined. They range from the dominant ethnic group, the Pashtuns to the isolated groups such as the artisans in tribal zones, who have only a negative identity, for they are placed even lower than the lowest rung of the ethnic ladder. Since the last century, migrations, evictions and modifications occurring in the social structure itself have thrown the country into turmoil, especially in the northern part. The introduction of a market economy, the increase in population and the intervention of the state have all accentuated divisions within society and created the conditions for the emergence of a class of well-to-do property owners and entrepreneurs living around the towns. We should also distinguish between the tribal and the non-tribal zones, even if the line between the two is often blurred. Every Afghan is linked to the past by a line of ancestors traced back through his forefathers. He is also conscious of belonging to an entity, which takes the form of a more or less endogenous community (*Qawm*), whether its sociological basis is tribe, clan, professional group (*Qawm* of the mullahs or of *Barbers*), caste (the Bari of Nuristan), religious group (the *Sayyad*), ethnic group (*Munjam*), village community or simply an extended family. We will reserve the term 'tribe' (*Qabila*) for the *qawms* having traditional rights and customs, a system within Islam of autonomous values (honour, vengeance etc), and a complex of specific institutions. These are essentially the Pashtun zones of the east, where we find the *Pashtunwali* (which is at one and the same time both code and an ideology) and the institution of the *Jirga*, the assemblies of all the men in the tribe. Moreover, the great tribes (Mohmmand, Jadran, Jaji, etc.) have territorial bases. For the Pashtun of the west, essentially the Durrani, the case is more complex. There is certainly a tribal memory, in the sense that belonging to the tribe and the clan is something of which people are well aware and quite happy to talk about. Their allegiance is directed towards the great families, such as to respect the tribal mythology of the great *Jirga* and the principle of egalitarianism. However, Durrani tribal institutions are nothing like as strong as those of the tribes of the eastern part of the country, or those of the Ghilzai. On the other hand, the influence of the *Ulama* is stronger amongst the Durrani. It seems that the Durrani have never been conscious of their tribal affinities as people in the east; having a closer relationship with the structures of the state (Safavides, then the Amir of Kabul) they have, in a very short time, developed a kind of aristocracy reinforced by the lands gifted by the monarchy (the system of *Jagir*). Yet the Durrani form an integral part of the Pashtun tribal world, and are considered as its cradle. It is manipulated by legitimizing symbols, which were recognized as such by the peasants.

Since the state did not have at its disposal enough officials to be able to spread out from the capital and divide the countryside up neatly into administrative areas, it was obliged to delegate some of its functions to people of standing in the local community, who thus became intermediaries between the state and the people. By this, their power was enhanced and they became, in the eyes of the state, the representatives of their community. These people were not necessarily Khan, and their power was based on their wealth and the power of the *qawm*. They were more likely to be *malik* or *arbab*, terms sometimes translated as village chiefs; they represented, in fact, a local *qawm* (there could be several *maliks* per village) and were elected by heads of families. They received remuneration from the families they served, and sometimes a payment from the state, and in return they acted as registrars, dealing with census returns, conscription and the collection of taxes; they also assisted those within their administrative area in their dealings with the authorities. The position of the *maliks* was somewhat ambiguous, for they represented the state to the community and the community to the state; in the years immediately prior to the coup, they tended to use this ambiguity to strengthen their personal position. But they were considered by the peasants to be one of them. On the other hand, as far as the administration of justice was concerned, the state had embarked upon a course of systematically removing all their authority from the village assemblies, and the *Qazi* who were not appointed by the government were deprived of the right of making judgments.

Over the years, the symbols used by the state to legitimatize its authority have varied dimensions. The original symbol that of tribal legitimacy was, of course, only valid in tribal zones, especially those of the Durranis, and there it retained its force. It was in the name of tribal solidarity that Abdur Rahman asked the Durranis to people of northwestern Afghanistan. Later, Amanullah made an appeal from Kandahar in order to regain the throne in 1985. It was in the name of tribal solidarity that Nadir Khan retook Kabul from Bacha-yi Saqqao in 1929. In these cases, legitimacy was conferred by the ritual of enthronement carried out by the great *Jirga*. The second symbol of legitimacy consisted simply in the actual possession of power, since for the peasants, such power was automatic, and held to exist and because no one was attempting to gainsay it. The existence of the state was, therefore, not the issue, except its right to encroach upon the country. With the exception of the tribal zones and Hazarajat, Afghanistan has always been subject to a central power, whose legitimacy, ever since the Muslim conquest, has been symbolized by the minting of money and the *Khutba* (the Friday Sermon) in the name of the sovereign; the constitution of 1923, Article 7, ratified these two outward signs. It mattered little which individual became the incarnation of this de facto power (a question asked after the communist coup was: Is Taraki the new king?). The existence of the state is not what is at stake for the peasant, whose chief concern is to resist the encroachment of the state bureaucracy, which will endure whichever regime or sovereign is in power.

People

The Afghan population is heterogeneous with numerous ethnic groups and dialects. The largest ethnic people are the Pasthuns, followed by Tajiks, Uzbeks and Hazaras respectively.[3] The original ethnic composition of Afghanistan was clearly dominated by the Pashtuns. During the Great Game between Britain and Russia in 19th century, the British encouraged successive Afghan rulers to push borders of Afghanistan to merge them as buffer state. Both Britishers as well as Russians had a policy to fragment Afghan territory at the hands of group leaders in the areas populated by Hazaras, Tajiks, Uzbeks and other non-Pashtuns to maintain their supremacy into the region as whole.[4] This state of affairs led to a continuous confrontation with Pakistan and also complicated the efforts to find peace in the post-Soviet Afghanistan.

The civil war in Afghanistan affected the demography of Afghanistan negatively. Most of the refugees were found in the south of the country were Pashtuns, while those taking refuge in Afghanistan as a result of civil war in Tajikistan were Tajiks. As such, chaotic situation and disorder prevailed in the country having adverse effect culminating into group rivalry, which ultimately resulted in formation of tribal society.

Another significant fact with far-reaching political and sociological implications on the Afghan ethnic scene was the overflow of all the major ethnic groups into neighbouring states: the Pashtuns into Pakistan, and the Tajiks, Uzbeks and Turkmens into Tajikistan, Uzbekistan and Turkmenistan respectively. All these groups had strong cultural, economic and more importantly, political affinity with their ethnic cousins across the borders. It is interesting to note that there are more Pashtuns in Pakistan now than in Afghanistan and there are more Tajiks in Afghanistan than in Tajikistan.

Islam is the predominant religion of Afghanistan (more then 99 per cent of the population is Muslim). The vast majority (about 85 per cent are Sunni Muslims, while the rest are mainly Shias with few Ismailis). Majority of the Shias take religious and political inspiration from revolutionary Iran, while the Pashtuns have traditionally been the main proponents of the 'Pasthtunism Cause'– the main bone of contention between Pakistan and Afghanistan. Ironically, the Pashtuns, who are part of the present Afghan power struggle, are the best bet of Pakistani interests in that country. Even the Pashtun dominated Taliban had not publicly recognized the Durand Line. Afghanistan has always been at the crossroads and succumbed to turmoil. Influence of great powers at different stages of history had kept the Afghans in a state of tension and confusion as a result of which, the economic, political and social structure of the country has been jeopardized.

The Afghan National Character

The absence of any serious demand for secession by any of many ethnic groups within Afghanistan expresses a great deal about the Afghan national character. Though the role of ethnicity in Afghanistan's internal or external situation cannot be downplayed, all Afghans feel strongly about their identity as Afghans. This characteristic becomes more significant when one takes into account the general international attitude towards national self-determination. Even during the Cold War era, they all faced the challenges of life bravely and did not allow the foreign traders to erode their culture and ethnicity. It is evident that despite war and turmoil, economic disruptions and political instability in Afghanistan could not deter the Afghan people from maintaining their national identity.

In spite of the ten years of Soviet occupation and the ongoing infighting among *Mujahideen* around Kabul, most parts of the country were free of both foreign interference and *Mujahideen* dictatorship. Throughout history, Afghans have also proven that they have a very low level of tolerance towards foreign domination and any kind of interference in their internal affairs. External powers much stronger than Pakistan, Iran, and Saudi Arabia have regretted their uninvited interference in Afghanistan. To any casual observer, Afghan's contempt for foreign domination has not changed much in the past two centuries. In 1879, exactly 100 years before the Soviet occupation of Afghanistan, when the British forces occupied parts of Afghanistan for the second time in 40 years, General Robert concluded that suspicion and hatred towards foreigners were too important and intense to be ignored and observed. Amir Abdur Rahman Khan who had spent years in Russia as an honoured quest of the Tsar, wrote of his gratitude to the Russians and loyalty to that country and its people. Even though the Allied Powers had always kept Afghans in a state of war and turmoil-still Afghans had not lost their inherited hospitality. It is an absolute historical fact that the kindness and behavioural attitude of the Afghans was remarkable. They were even kind to their enemies. One Russian General writes, "Personally I am under great allegiance to the Afghan people and shall never forget their kindness, because ingratitude is the very worst of the sins."

The Post-1945 Era

Post-imperialist era Afghans faced the dilemma of balancing the needs of development and concerns for security; they had to choose between their state closed and inaccessible to outside influences, and the need and desire to develop, which required opening up of foreign policy with better economic policy. But outside influences were always keeping Afghans in a state of turmoil and these Afghan people were never in a position to maintain political and economic stability. Afghans turned to the United States for help in this regard.

The American response to Afghan's needs was, however, cold and negative. Despite negative response, Afghans went ahead by signing agreement with a private American company for the construction of modern highways and repair of existing irrigation dams and building some new canals in the territory of Afghanistan. Afghanistan has three outlets, through Iran in the west, through the Soviet Union and Pakistan, which have been heavily used. The Iranian railhead at Mashad is about 1,195 miles from Herat. The Soviet railroad at Kushka is 65 miles north of Herat and Mazar-i-Sharif in northern Afghanistan is near two branches of the Soviet railroad at Termez. The Pakistani railway at Quetta lies 130 miles south of Kandahar, and that at Peshawar lies 75 miles south of Jalalabad. Afghanistan's needs for the Pakistani route are due to the legal import and export transit trade through Karachi. The illegal smuggling of various luxury goods that are imported for Afghanistan but are really for re-shipment to the Pakistani markets. Pakistan has occasionally used this Afghan reliance to exert political pressure on . Since its inception, Pakistan had to contend with demands for a Pashtun state. Afghanistan's southern routes were blocked, access was sporadically denied to the port of Karachi. Pakistan, thereby, attempted to strengthen its grip on the Afghan economy and politics. The repeated closure of the Afghan-Pakistan border prompted the Afghans to consider alternative routes in order to decrease, and finally to end its dependence on Pakistan. This led to a redirection of Afghanistan's economy and politics towards its northern part. This also contributed to a mutual mistrust between the people and policy makers of the two neighbours. Mindful of the Soviet Union's unreliability and its historic tendency to expand southwards, the Afghans observed that actions were always motivated by their own interests. However, they assumed Soviet planners to be reasonable, whose interests could be hampered by an attack on Afghanistan. They argued that Afghanistan would be an economic liability and to control it would be difficult and costly, and most importantly, any such aggression would have disastrous repercussions on the neutralist nations in Asia and Africa.

The Great Game continued even after 1945 and United States retained an active role in world politics after World War II. Its role revolved mainly around the policy of containment of communism. The United States gradually eased out the former colonial powers from the world stage, as these empires crumbled. The British, having left the sub-continent in 1947, was no longer in the Great Game. Although the Great Game continued, there were different players and the way it was played, was entirely different. The American view of Afghanistan was of a small state with no or very insignificant strategic value, especially when compared to Pakistan. The United States of America did not pay any heed to repeated Afghan requests for arms, while those for economic aid were responded to only as a reaction to the Soviet aid and influence. Despite indications that continuing negation of Afghan requests would open a window of opportunity for the Soviet Union, the United States remained insensitive to the regional politics in Afghanistan. It insisted that Afghanistan should mend fences with Pakistan in affairs of the region. Such an American policy was not acceptable for the Afghan political set up. A policy review in 1971 cited the US objectives in Afghanistan that included improvement of relations with Pakistan and Iran, and providing help to establish a political and economic system in Afghanistan.

To set the record straight, Afghanistan was invited to join the Baghdad Pact, but it was not accepted by the Afghans, believing that it would bring her into direct conflict with the Soviet Union and would violate its traditional and time-tested policy of neutrality. The Afghan attempts to get the US help were not meant to annoy Soviet Union, and place itself at the mercy of a distant friend. The real intentions were to find support and understanding from the global rival of the Soviet Union, to shed isolation and buffer status, considered necessary for development, but still retain its independence. The Unites States, then involved in the Cold War could not appreciate the worries of a small and insignificant state like Afghanistan. To the America of those days, any talk of non-alignment and nationalism was equal to being at least on the side of communism. Accordingly, Afghanistan remained in a state of constant tension and was not in a position to devise its economic and political policy. Internal conflicts continued and their struggle for balancing the needs of development and concern for security could not maintain the momentum.

Failure of the United States to satisfy Afghan expectations gave an opening to the Soviet Union. The increasing ties between Pakistan and the United States were seen with suspicion in Kabul. In 1956, the South East Asia Treaty Organization (SEATO), the South Asian extension of containment, endorsed Pakistan's position on the Durand Line. In 1954, when the United States' plan to arm Pakistan's became known, a major breakthrough in Soviet-Afghan relations took place. There was no economically feasible transit route across Iran, but Soviet railroad reached the north bank of the Amu Darya. In July 1950, the Soviet Union signed a four-year trade agreement with Afghanistan to barter Soviet petroleum, cotton, fruit, sugar and other commodities for Afghan wool, furs, raw cotton, fruits and nuts. It also provided duty free transit for Afghan goods. Soviet Union also started expressing sympathy with Pashtunistan. Afghanistan's favourable tilt towards the Soviet Union that had started in the 1950s culminated in the Soviet physical take over of Afghanistan in 1979.

For all practical purposes during the Cold War era, all diplomatic and political signals to Moscow from the West indicated that Americans were aware of the strategic significance of Afghanistan and were accordingly trying to make their base in Afghanistan. The Soviet intervention in Afghanistan created a swift but strong reaction across the world. It put the Soviet Union on the defensive before the outrage of the international community. Not only the Western world, but also the Third World countries condemned the Soviet action. In the special General Assembly Session in January 1980, ten states voted in favour of the resolution condemning the Soviet Union. The number kept increasing every year until the withdrawal of the Soviet Union in 1988-89. The Americans suddenly realized the centrality of Afghanistan to the Middle East, South Asia and West Asia. Due to its location, it provided the Soviets access to the Middle East (Gulf region) and South Asia. The strategic significance of this fact of geography prompted a reaction that is known as the "Carter Doctrine." Pakistan under military dictatorship wanted to make itself useful and to prevail upon Afghanistan Pakistan and the Unites States found a strategic congruity in opposition to Soviet control of Afghanistan and the threat that this intervention posed to security in the Gulf, South Asia and Middle East. Pakistan became the third largest recipient of both military and economic aid after Israel and Egypt. The Russian plan to prop up the communist government in Afghanistan and suppress the resistance with force failed abysmally. The Soviet Union collapsed as a state in 1991, the reasons for that historic change that has irrevocably changed the face of international politics were many, with the Afghan resistance being one of these.

As a result of that collapse, five new Muslim states in Central Asia emerged. They are, however, still tied with Russia through Commonwealth of Independent States (CIS). How much Russia still controls the policies of these Republics may be difficult to assess at this stage. From the history of nations, one learns that history and geography determines a state's foreign and security policy. Russians have historically considered the control of its southern Asian landmass as critical to its security. The northern tier is fast becoming the Russian dominated Commonwealth's (CIS) southern tier.[13] Afghanistan is the southern border of that southern tier.

Post-Cold War Era

In the post-Soviet withdrawal period, the former communist regime of the People's Democratic Party of Afghanistan (PDPA), renamed as the *Watan Party*, continued to rule over Afghanistan. That government collapsed in 1992, when President Najibullah agreed to step down as a result of a UN-brokered peace plan. The UN peace plan, however, could not take off because Ahmad Shah Masood (a Tajik and the most celebrated and well known resistance leader) with the help of Rashid Dostum (an Uzbek and a well-known communist General) took over Kabul.

There were many outside powers and Afghan resistance groups with different and often conflicting agendas for a future Afghanistan. Besides the immediate neighbours i.e. Pakistan, Iran, and the former Soviet Central Asian Republics plus Russia, these powers included countries ranging from Saudi Arabia to Turkey, India as well as the USA.

Pakistan, the main route of international support for the Afghan resistance, considered itself better placed and positioned to reap the benefits of this new situation. Pakistani strategists had their own agendas, primarily Targeting at India. It was believed that Pakistan would get some weapons plus the so called 'strategic depth' out of the situation that had arisen in Afghanistan. With a friendly government installed in Kabul, Pakistan neither had to worry about the Pashtunistan[5] problem nor the close Indo-Afghan ties. Pakistan's policy towards Afghanistan defined by General Zia-ul-Haq in the late 1970s and 1980s continued to hold sway despite the end of martial law in 1988. Pakistan's basic objectives were to weaken the Afghan state, which since 1947 had favoured an alliance with India. Pakistan's military and political support to Hizb-i-Islam contributed to the destabilization of Afghanistan, which undermines Pakistan's pretensions to play an important role in post-communist Central Asia. Pakistani authorities have long been uncertain about the kind of state they would prefer to see emerge in Afghanistan, but many of Pakistan's leaders harbour a deep-rooted suspicion about Afghan intentions in the post-war period. The civil war in Afghanistan gave Pakistan an opportunity to influence events in Afghanistan beyond its expectations. It has continuously been trying to regain imitative which it had lost with its inability to control *Mujahideen* groups.

Pakistan's inability to control Gulbudin Hekmatyar, once considered as Pakistan's most preferred resistance commander and the top recipient of international military aid via Pakistan, led to Pakistan's attempt to change its strategy from time to time. Pakistan supported a weak and moderate resistance leader, Mojaddidi as President of Afghanistan after Najibullah's ouster in 1992. By bringing Prof. Rabbani to Afghan power struggle, who replaced Mojaddidi, Pakistan again played a decisive role. Once installed, neither of them could fulfil Pakistani expectations. Probably both were thinking like Amir Abdur Rahman Khan a century earlier. The new force, the Taliban, who have taken Afghanistan by storm after their sudden appearance in late 1992 are widely believed to have the active support of Pakistan. While Prof. Rabbani's government and the anti-Taliban Alliance-and even most independent observers claim the Pakistan-Taliban link, both the Taliban and Pakistan denied any such relationship.[6] The alleged Pakistani attempts to impose a peace of its choice on Afghanistan have given a chance to both India and Russia to re-enter Afghanistan. Taliban success can be directly attributed to Pakistani support and failure of the Afghans to realize that Taliban are supported by external forces.

Iran is a neighbour with vital interests in what happens in Afghanistan. Iran is a Muslim state dominated by Shia community. Though this factor limits her ability to influence events in Afghanistan, which is largely a Sunni Muslim dominated state, it has not stopped her from influencing Afghan politics. Even if Persian-speaking Tajiks and other non-Pashtuns do not share the religious beliefs of Iran, they welcome Iran's support. Iranian interest in Afghan territory was to make its Shiite ideology to prevail there.

The visit of Iranian Deputy Foreign Minister Alladudin Bourajerdi to the northern provinces of Afghanistan, shows the involvement and interests of Iran in Afghan Affairs.[7] At the same time, Uzbeks, Tajiks, Russians and Indians have been trying to stop Afghanistan from maintaining relations with Pakistan.

The importance of Afghanistan has increased in the post-Cold War era. From being a buffer state during the Great Game to a significant small state in the backyard of the Soviet Union, it has become a centre of strategic importance for many external actors. Russians took control of Central Asia long before 1917. Afghanistan was left out not because the Russians were disinterested, but because of the British resistance. Russians had historically considered the control of its southern Asian neighbourhood. Russian interest in Afghanistan is evident from her continued interest in Central Asia. Russia has never denied her continued interest in Central Asia and Afghanistan. Russians had shown and are showing an active interest in what happens in Kabul.[8] Afghanistan is the key to Central Asia. The significance of Central Asia needs no emphasis. Central Asia is world's second richest source of energy after the Middle East besides being a rich source of precious metals and minerals. The breakup of the Soviet Union has unleashed a new struggle for access to and outlets for Central Asia. The five Central Asian Republics as well as the rest of the world are in search of alternative access routes to the energy resources. At a time when the world economy is in dire need of new energy sources, the significance of these Republics increases. Free market interests would be served best by giving substance to the sovereignty of these new Republics. The key to translate their new-found sovereignty into reality lies in decreasing dependence on Russia. One of the most essential requirements for such independence to materialize is finding alternate access to the world markets. Turkey through Azerbaijan, Georgia or Iran, and Pakistan through Afghanistan and/or Iran are the alternative access routes. Although for the Western countries, Turkey appears to be the best choice, Afghanistan via Pakistan, is economical, and the best and shortest access route to the high seas and the world markets. Strategically, it would be best for the world economy and the Central Asian states to have freedom of choice. In this line of argument, the West cannot ignore even Iran[9] (See Table 1).

Afghanistan provides two outlets to Central Asia, one through Pakistan and the other through Iran. Both these routes need to be opened and developed. The pre-feasibility report of the proposed railway line between Pakistan and Turkmenistan opens up the possibility of three routes through Afghanistan and Pakistan.

Table–1
Railroad Distance

Dushanbe and Vladivostok	9,500 kms
Dushanbe and Rostov Na Donu	4,200 kms

Source: The Daily Muslim, Islamabad, 7 November 1993.

Central Asia and other outside powers, who are interested to have access to the region, would not be dependent on any one party. These would forestall the replay of the Great Game, which resulted in the Russia control of Central Asia. The British could only take a defensive position through manoeuvering of Afghan politics, boundaries and routes during the old Great Game. The aim was to deny Russians any access to India and the Persian Gulf, a policy dictated by the imperial interests of the nineteenth century. Today's geopolitics demands the opening of new routes. The instability in Russia and her renewed appreciation of the historic southward expansion increases the significance of Afghanistan.[10]

For Central Asia to evolve as a truly independent region, the role of Afghanistan would be crucial. One fact of history and geography must be clear i.e., Russia will always have an interest and influence in that region. An outside approach to the region must take account of the legitimate Russian interests. The interest of the world economy and security is not in animosity and conflict between Central Asia and Russia. However, the world cannot afford to let Russia have exclusive control of or access to the region and its resources. They would be suicidal not to decrease the dependence of Central Asia on Russia and conversely ease the access of the global market access to it. When one talks of Central Asia, one should not be concerned only with the former Soviet Union and/or Russia, but with a region or regions that exist outside as well.

The ease of communications in post-imperialist Central Asia means that Afghanistan now has no choice but to interact with each other directly. They will certainly be mirrors of each other, whether they like it or not. Their similarities in their histories and recent past-problems in their relationships with outside world, in regional interactions, in the reconstruction of political legitimacy, in relations between their Islamic character and their desire for modernity, and the establishment of internal peace and stability may well encourage them to serve each other as they begin to face the realities of the coming century.[11]

The potential of the Afghan crisis to spread out in the region is clearly manifested in its location and ethnic composition. An extension of the process of ethnic breakup, already sparked by the formation of new Republics in Central Asia, could indirectly lead to such developments as the breakaways of ethnically related northern Afghanistan to join Central Asian neighbours. The breakup of Afghanistan would then provoke ethnic struggles in Pakistan, Iran and the northwestern border areas of China.[12] Even India may not remain untouched by such happenings in Afghanistan.

In the nineteenth century, Afghanistan emerged as a buffer state between the contending British Indian and Tsarist Russian colonial empires. This overwhelmingly Muslim (more than 99 per cent), landlocked nation covers an area of 647,500 square kilometers consisting of rugged mountains, deep valleys, deserts and arid plateaus. Situated in the heart of Asia, it has been an important crossroads for diverse people and their cultural and religious traditions.[13] Neither the actual size nor the ethnic composition of the population is known because no complete national census has ever been taken. In 1986-87, the United Nations High Commission for Refugees (UNHCR) estimated the total population at 16.7 million, with 11 million living inside Afghanistan, and 5.7 million who were then refugees (2.4. million in Iran, 3.2 million in Pakistan and one million in other parts of the world). Since April 1992, following the collapse of the Soviet installed Najibullah government, the refugees have flocked to rural areas and provincial towns. Continuing factional fighting[14] among the Afghan *Mujahideen* (Islamist resistance groups) for control of Kabul has resulted in further displacement of hundreds of thousands of people, most of them to Pakistan.

Estimates of the proportions of ethnic groups (based on language and sectarian affiliation) in Afghanistan are highly contested and increasingly politicized. In the early 1970s, Afghan expert Louis

Dupree offered the following estimates: Pashtun 47 per cent, Tajik-Farsiwan-Airmaq 35 per cent, Uzbek, Turkmen, and Kirghiz eight per cent, Hazara seven per cent, Baluch-Barahui 2.5 per cent and other Muslim and non-Muslim groups, including Hindus, Sikhs, and Jews, 0.5 per cent. Based on Dupree's estimates, Sunnis constitute 88 per cent and Shias (primarily Imami and some Islmaili) 12 per cent of the Muslim population. Dupree used official information provided by the Pashtun-dominated government and assumed the total population to be about 14 million. At present, by contrast, the Shia political groups claim that Shia constitute 20 to 25 per cent of the national population and are demanding proportional representation.[15]

Historically, Muslim Arab armies penetrated the region at the turn of the eighth century AD. Many Muslim empires rose in this area during the following centuries and expanded the frontiers of Islam into Central and South Asia. Modern Afghanistan is the remnant of the Durrani empire founded by Ahmad Shah Durrani (1747-1772), one of the last such great Muslim empires in the region. The Durrani empire began to disintegrate at the turn of the nineteenth century owing to bloody struggles over succession as well as growing external military and political pressures. The prolonged fratricidal wars (1800-80) encouraged British and Russian colonial bosses. These civil wars and colonial interventions resulted in the increasing economic, military and technological dependence of Afghan governments on European colonial and post-colonial powers.

The effects of foreign assistance and interventions began immediately after the second Anglo-Afghan War (1879-80), when Britain installed Amir Abdur Rahman Khan (1880-1901), a member of the Muhammadzai branch of the Durranis. With substantial annual British subsidies and technical assistance, Amir Abdur Rahman, who was known as the 'Iron Amir," consolidated power over the entire country.[16] Unlike his predecessors, Amir Abdur Rahman believed that his power as Amir emanated directly from the God rather than from the support of the people or tribal Khans. He took the title *Zi'ul Millat-i-Wal-Din* (Light of the Nation and the Faith) and claimed that God's purpose in honouring him with His "Vice-Regency" was to avert the threat of foreign aggression against Afghanistan and to safeguard it from further internal disturbances.

He forcibly converted the people of Kafristan, the only remaining indigenous non-Muslim in the country, and renamed their territory Nuristan (Land of Light). In an attempt to pacify the recalcitrant Hazara Shias of Central Afghanistan, he labelled them infidels and declared a *ghazawat* or *Jihad* against them.

The 'Iron Amir' justified his cruel policies by systematically dressing the monarchy in an Islamic cloth. As head of an Islamic state, the Amir claimed to be the sole interpreter if religious doctrine, and proclaimed that "whether just or despotic, the King must be obeyed, provided his commands do not violate the *Shariat*. Suspected enemies were killed, exiled, or detained in the capital, or their young sons were held hostage as *ghulam bachagan* (court page boys). The Amir's disingenuous use of Islam in this manner was not without precedent. His policies differed only in the rigorous articulation and effective utilization of the main operative principles of Afghan political culture, ideals of kingship, kinship[17] and Islam, buttressed by patron client and primonial practices and by politics of fear and favour (*zur ya zar*). He weakened the pervasive role of *Ulama* and *mashayikh* (Sufi leaders) in the management of Islamic education and civil society and claimed these tasks for the state. Administration of *Awqaf* (Muslim endowments, waqf) and Muslim education were incorporated into the state apparatus. *Shariat* court disputes outside the state courts were forbidden. For the first time in the history of the country, books of sermons and guidelines for preaching were published and widely disseminated, many of these were still used in the *masjid jami* (Great Mosques) in Afghanistan today. Tribal stratification among the Pashtun, as well as sectarian inequalities favouring Sunnis over Shias and Pashtuns over non-Pashtuns, were institutionalized. The peasantry in general and those in non-Pashtun areas in particular suffered oppressive taxation. Villages replaced tribal and ethnic communities as principal units of administration. These policies produced alienation and resignation among large segments of the rural population, giving rise to the development of smaller, village based, parallel power structures that enabled the villagers to limit costly contact with state maintained unchanged during the reign of his son, Amir Habib Allah (1890-1919).[18]

Towards the end of Habib Allah's reign, with the introduction of modern schools and the press, new political ideals as constitutionalism, nationalism, liberal, secularism, reformism and Islamic modernism were incorporated in the political culture of Afghanistan, both tc complement and to compete with the traditional ideals of kinship and Islam. These ideals found adherents among the nascent intelligentsia, members of the royal family, the court page boys, and some *Ulamas*. King Amanullah (1919-29), one of the grandsons of Amir Abdur Rahman and a supporter of modernist-nationalist thought, introduced the first constitution of Afghanistan (1923). He attempted to promote the idea of equality and the development of a national ideology based on traits common to all citizens of Afghanistan, but he failed. His rule was challenged by a popular armed rebellion supported by some conservative *Ulamas* and *ruhanis* (spiritual of Sufi dignitaries), under the banner of *Jihad* against an "infidel king", and he was forced into exile in 1929.[19]

Muhammad Nadir Shah (ruled from 1929-33), who succeeded King Amanullah after a nine-month interregnum, attributed his success to "the exclusive help of the Almighty God" and the "sacrifices of the people of Afghanistan." Nadir Shah abandoned many of Amanullah's Western-inspired reforms and attempted to legitimize his own dynastic rule through constitutional means. He called a Grand Assembly (*Loya Jirga*) or the tribal elders, religious dignitaries, and local aristocrats to ratify a new constitution (1931). He established a *Jamiat-ul-Ulama* (Supervisory Council of Muslim Scholars), ordered the first printing of the holy Quran in the country and removed restrictions on the role of the mullahs and *moulvis* (Muslim scholars) in education, reaffirmed the absolute primacy of *Hanafi Shariat* in the country. He closed girls' schools and formally sanctioned gender inequalities. Reverting to Amir Abdur Rahman's practices, both civil and criminal cases were brought within the domain of *Shariat* courts, making them the most important vehicles of centralization. Pashtun tribes in the southeastern frontier, who had helped him in his bid for power, were granted exemptions from taxes and conscription, and members of the influential Mojaddidi family of *ruhanis* were awarded cabinet posts for their support. Discrimination against non-Pashthuns became rampant in the allocation of economic, educational and developmental resources. Many rural aristocrats were co-opted by the Musahiban monarchy by being either elected to or selected for the newly established rubber stamp bicameral parliament (*Majilis-Shura wa A'yan*).

The Musahiban rulers (1929-1978) pursued ambivalent policies towards Islam especially in expanding modern educational system. Islam was presented in the curriculum simply as a body of rituals and legal injunctions rather than as a vibrant religious doctrine compatible with modern living. The educational system had a secularist agenda devoid of any coherent or viable moral and political processes, nation building and the so called modernization programmes in the form of *Demokrasii*. Now (New Democracy) turned out to be nothing more than a few staged "democratic" procedures, such as voting for rubber-stamp parliaments, and a "free" press. Therefore, during the crucial decades of the 1960s, when economic development programs were failing and development-related corruption was rampant, Afghan leaders became preoccupied with introducing Western style governance to appease their foreign patrons, instead of extending social services and equitably meeting the needs of all citizens.

After the promulgation of the liberal constitution of 1964 and the onset of New Democracy in Afghanistan, Marxist and Maoist parties were formed. In response, Islamist movements began to emerge, not only to address the potential communist threat but also to challenge the legitimacy of the Musahiban monarchy. The rise of both communist and Islamist parties and movements-each with ideological ties and financial patrons (actual or potential) outside the country-was without precedent in the political history of Afghanistan. The government's dependence on foreign and the maintenance of its large military and police forces had also reached new heights.

Specifically, the Afghan state banked overwhelmingly on Soviet patronage for its survival. Hence the government strongly opposed the Islamist movements, while the communist groups, especially the pro Soviet Marxist parties, were given free rein. As a consequence, in July 1973 Prince Muhammad Daud, a former Prime Minister (from 1953 to 1963) and also a longtime loyal supporter of the pro-Soviet Marxists, staged a military coup, abolished the monarchy, and proclaimed himself President of the Republic of Afghanistan (1973-78). Only five years later, Daud himself was ousted by a coup led by the People's Democratic Party of Afghanistan (PDPA) that ended Durrani dynasty's rule by establishing a communist government (1978-1992). The Islamist movements, already seriously weakened by the monarchy and Daud's regime, suffered devastating new attacks from the Marxist government. Ironically, the usurpation of state power by the PDPA offered the fledgling Islamist movements a new lease on life.

Islamist revolutionary ideas were brought to Afghanistan from Egypt in the 1950s by a new Afghan scholar studying at al-Azhar University in Cairo (Egypt) and by al-Azhar Sheikhs teaching at the Faculty of *Shariat* (Islamic Studies) at Kabul University. The Islamist political movement emerged on the campus of Kabul University, initially with an underground faculty wing and a public student branch, the Nahzat-i-Javanan-i-Muslim (Muslim Youth Movement). Unlike earlier rural centered *Jihad* movements mobilized exclusively to oppose outside colonial forces or the allegedly un-Islamic policies of a particular ruler, the new Islamist movement was urban-centred, organized and led by educated youth who questioned the legitimacy of the existing political system, and it called for the positive radical transformation of power relations through the establishment of an Islamic government. The Islamist movement attracted mostly provincial and rural youth who were studying in Kabul and other major towns. Before the Marxist coup, they had few active supporters among traditionally educated *ulama* and mashaikh, especially in the rural areas. However, following the PDPA coup, elements of the Islamist groups living in exile in Pakistan and elsewhere quickly joined with traditional tribal and religious leaders in rural areas to launch a nationwide popular armed struggle, a *Jihad* that eventually drove out the invading Soviet army (1989), defeated the Afghan communists, and declared Afghanistan an Islamic state (April, 1992).

Their apparent military triumph, however, has gradually deteriorated into humiliating and bloody inter-ethnic and sectarian warfare. The vastly popular Islamist armed struggle, despite its remarkable military success, did not produce a coherent Islamic ideology or political and ideological defeat, which raised serious doubts about the future viability of militant Islamist political struggles. This is especially true in the minds of those educated Muslim youth who were a ray of hope after the Afghan *Mujahideen* became triumphant.

The tensions currently undermining the *Mujahideen* are rooted in the recent history of Islamist movements in Afghanistan. The *Jihad* struggle was spearheaded and sustained by two major factions of the original Islamist movement, the *Jamiat-i-Islami* (Islamic Society) headed by Burhanuddin Rabbani, an al-Azhar educated former Professor of Islamic Studies, and the *Hizb-i-Islami* (Islamic Party) led by Gulbuddin Hekmatyar, a former undergraduate engineering student at Kabul University. The split in the *Ikhwan-al-Muslimin* (Muslim Brotherhood) movement in Egypt was reflected in this factional difference. Rabbani favoured Hassan al-Banna's moderate populist approach seeking to effect change from the bottom up. Hekmatyar, by contrast, favoured the more radical strategies of Sayyid Qutb and his more militant followers, the Hijirat was al-Takfir faction led by Umar Abd al-Rahman that called for change from the above through capturing state power.

The impact of these differences in Rabbani and Hekmatyar's political outlooks combined with their distinct ethnic affiliations (Rabbani is a Tajik and Hekmatyar a Pashtun) and serious inter-personal tensions became evident when the two leaders took refuge in Pakistan. In the economically and politically volatile environment of the Afghan exile community in Peshawar, animosities and factional conflicts increased.

Two other developments also played a significant role in the creation and perpetuation of factional divisions within the *Jihad* movements in Afghanistan. First, the Pakistan government created and officially recognized five additional, primarily Pashtun-dominated resistance organizations. These groups included two led by traditional *ulama* (Moulvi Yunus Khalis and Moulvi Muhammad Nabi Muhammadi), two by *ruhani* families (Sibghat Allah Mojaddidi and Sayyid Ahmad Gilani) with strong ties to the defunct monarchy, and one led by another al-Azhar educated former Kabul University Professor, Abd al-Rabb Rasul Sayyaf. In addition, at least eight Shia resistance groups were organized in Iran and one in Pakistan. The Iranian groups have formed an alliance called *Ali Wahdat-i-Islami* (Islamic Unity) led by Muhammad Ali Mazari. Scores of other non-official *Mujahideen* groups active in the resistance completed these groups.

Second, nearly all these groups, both Muslim and non-Muslim, were or still are headquartered in neighbouring Pakistan and Iran and are completely dependent on outside sources, for money and arms. Because of direct Soviet intervention, there were no shortages of foreign supporters, both covert and overt, especially during the

Reagan era, to help defeat and destroy the erstwhile USSR. *Mujahideen* parties and organizations representing many diverse (ideological, sectarian, ethno-linguistic, tribal, regional and local) interest groups competed with one another for the patronage of numerous international aid organizations.

The reason for the political and ideological failure of the *Mujahideen* was the fact that their numerous foreign patrons gradually but systematically subordinated the Islamist ideological purpose of *Jihad* to their own anti-communist and anti-Soviet military objectives. Therefore, as soon as Soviet troops withdrew, external sponsors drastically reduced support to the *Mujahideen* and even encouraged factional fighting to undermine their Islamic fundamentalist aims and objectives.

Undoubtedly, both the role of Islam in Afghan politics and the *Mujahideen* commitment to Islamist ideology faced their most serious test after their military victory. Specifically, when an arrangement between the forces of Ahmad Shah Masud, a Tajik *Mujahideen* commander, and Abd al- Rashid Dostam, powerful Uzbek leader of a militia force in northern Afghanistan, brought about the collapse of Dr. Najibullah's Marxist government in Kabul, the *Mujahideen* had a chance to end the war and establish an Islamic government. They failed because of powerful feelings of mistrust, encouraged by their foreign patrons, among the factions.

On the fall of the communist regime, the forces of the Iranian-backed Islamic Unity coalition of eight Shia and other predominantly Hazara groups had occupied significant areas of Kabul. Dostam, forming and leading the National Islamic Movement of Northern Afghanistan (*Junbush-i-milli-i Islami Shimali Afghanistan*), demanded a role in the new Islamic state of Afghanistan. Similarly, other armed and newly empowered ethnic and sectarian minorities, such as the traditionally oppressed Shia, asked for fair representation in the new government.

Pashtun groups, notably those led by Sayyaf and Hekmatyar, responded by arms attacks against Masud, Dostam, and the Shia coalition forces in and around Kabul. Sayyaf, who enjoyed the support of powerful Saudi patrons, introduced controversial Wahabi practices and began armed attacks against the pro Iranian Shia Islamic Unity Group. Hekmatyar, formerly willing to recruit Pashtun communist officers from his failed military coups against the communist regime, condemned Ahmad Shah Masud's alliance with Rashid Dostam's militia in the government while welcoming numerous high-ranking communist Pashtun military officers into his own camp. Hekmatyar's devastating rocket attack against Kabul was apparently motivated by the fear that non-Pashtun minorities dominate the Central Government.

The present succession crisis has extensive historical precedents. Many Afghan leaders had employed Islam to manage kingship, kinship and ethnicity in order to further two often contradictory state goals: *(i)* to universalize, homogenize and integrate the diverse elements of society; and *(ii)* to differentiate and divide groups. Leaders used Islam as a unifying force most effectively in confrontation with non-Muslim forces offensively in the Durrani empire's expansionary wars in northern India, and defensively in *Jihads* against the Sikhs and the British in the nineteenth century, and more recently against the Afghan communities and the Soviets. Though a positive and constructive relationship between Islam and the political independence and integrity of the country has emerged with these experiences, there have been heightened feelings of xenophobia. Besides, there have been opportunities for political and military leadership of the local Khans. However, this development has generally worked against the domestic centralizing aims of the Afghan state.

At the domestic level, monarchs who deployed Islam to legitimize a policy of divide and rule could not consolidate power and war, which later told upon the nation building process. At the national level, the most significant examples are the Shia Sunni riots in Kabul in the first decade of the nineteenth century and Amir Abd al-Rahman's war against the Shias and Hazaras of central Afghanistan. At the local level, conflicts among tribal and ethnic communities (and at present among rival *Mujahideen* political parties and factions), or even among individuals, often escalated as moral conflicts being justified on Islamic grounds and arousing intense emotion. Conflicts between Pashtuns and Hazaras as well as among Hazaras and Sunni Tajiks and Uzbeks in northern Afghanistan (Turkistan) during the nineteenth century were the examples of ethnic wars that were translated into *Jihad*. Afghan government and its outside patrons have perpetuated communal tensions in pursuit of political advantage.

From the perspective of Afghan citizens, the legitimacy of governments (*hukumat*) and the state (*dawlat*) has always been contingent upon the responsibility of the state as a defender of Islam and the country, and also on the people's perception of the personal piety and dignity of the rulers and government officials. Periods of popular support coincided with the reigns of kings, who were considered pious and just (such as Ahmad Shah Durrani) or the leaders who were directly engaged in defence of Islam and the nation. Popular opposition arose when the personal integrity and piety of the ruler and his officials were questioned, and the sincerity and ability of the government to defend Islam were in doubt. The revolt against Amanullah and the recent *Jihad* against Khalq-Parcham Marxists and their Soviet protectors are the most obvious examples.

The participation of so many international actors, Muslim and non-Muslim, during the armed resistance against the Soviets has had a mixed outcome for the Islamist movements of Afghanistan. Outside patrons of *Jihad* helped the *Mujahideen* win a military victory. These patrons also engaged, directly or indirectly in fanning the flames of ethnic and sectarian conflicts in post-communist Afghanistan. Sadly, the flames of factional war have consumed not only Kabul but also the credibility of the Islamic ideology and the hopes and aspirations of millions of Muslims world wide.

Although the modern state structure of Afghanistan emerged in 1747 AD when Ahmad Shah Abdali unified different autonomous tribes to give the country a definite shape, yet Tsarist Russia subjected it to pressure by pushing ruthlessly down from the north and imperial British began to move towards its east. Now the main interest of the Afghan authorities was to avoid any collusion of Russia and Britain on Afghan soil. Right from the ancient history, Soviet Central Asia has played its part. Their intervention was with regard to their own interests which were mainly confined to achieve territorial expansion. Russians maintained their illegal occupation on Afghanistan, which continued till recent times.

The first official contact between the imperial Britain and Afghanistan was made in 1809 AD, when a British mission under Elephantine was dispatched to Peshawar to discuss with the Amir of Afghanistan regarding measures of mutual defence against the so called Franco-Russian threat to British India and Afghanistan. A Treaty of Alliance was concluded by which both the countries pledged lasting friendship and agreed not to interfere in each others' internal affairs. However, the French dangers faded away when Napoleon Bonaparte broke with the Tsar. The relations between Russia and Britain improved for some years owing to the coalitions formed against Napoleon Bonaparte. But the diplomatic tussle between the East India Company and the Tsar continued, because Russia started making attempts to assert her influence in Iran, Afghanistan and the Central Asian Khanates. Between 1809 and 1836, Britain took no interest in the affairs of Afghanistan despite the Russian advance towards the Iranian border, which caused considerable anxiety to the British authorities. Britain was told that if she wanted peace with Russian, she should recognize the Russian interests in Asia.

Russian authorities understood well that the future of Russia lies in Asia. Russians even thought that the stronger their position in Central Asia, the weaker will be the British power in India and the more conciliatory she will be in Europe partly because of their exploitative policy which was more powerful. British authorities seriously thought of dominating the intervening media, especially Iran, Afghanistan, Central Asia and even China. Thus Afghanistan, which no doubt formed the heart of Asia, proved to be a powerful springboard for military and political penetration for both the rivals against each other.

In 1838 AD, Iranian army reinforced at the suggestion of Russia attempted to capture Herat. British officials were alarmed at the Russian encouragement to Iran to claim sovereignty over Herat and western Afghanistan. With this, the actual conflict between Russia and Britain for supremacy in Afghanistan was born. The British desired to have a strong Afghanistan to defend itself against Russia and Iran. For this, the British Foreign Office favoured a "Forward Policy." Afghanistan was, henceforth, considered as the 'frontier' of India, and no European national was to be allowed to carry on any commercial or political activity there or to interfere in its affairs.

No doubt the outbreak of the so called Indian policy served as an encouraging factor to the Russian activities in Central Asia. It was fortunate for the British that during the disturbances in India, the diplomatic negotiations had resulted in Anglo-Afghan Treaty of 1855 and 1857. After the Sepoy Mutiny in India, which was known as the first War of Indian Independence, British Indian government thought of non-intervention in the internal affairs of Afghanistan. A close relationship developed between the two countries, in spite of the fact that in 1855 and again in 1869, the Afghans tried and failed to obtain British commitment for future assistance and an unequivocal guarantee of support in case of external attack. It was through the British mediation that Russia recognized the Oxus as the northern boundary of Afghanistan. Once the British controlled the sea routes to India, their attention was naturally directed towards the land routes, and Afghanistan became the focus of their attention. Apart from political and economic interests, British authorities wanted to cultivate friendly relations and so called faithful alliance with Afghanistan to stop the Russian penetration into that country. Thus from 1863 AD onwards, British Indian authorities took less interest in the affairs of Afghanistan.

British Government urged the necessity of constituting Afghanistan as a neutral zone and to demarcate its northern boundaries. The Tsar replied that Russia looked upon Afghanistan as completely outside the sphere of its influence. The rapid Russian advance in Central Asia after 1865 AD created a sense of alarm in British circles. Russo-Afghan frontier had been very frequently modified and the process continued up to 20th century, although the Tsarist government had declared that the Asiatic frontiers of Russia were well defined. No doubt, it was an easy job for British or Tsarist Russian to capture Afghanistan. But none of the two imperialist powers wanted a confrontation with each other. So Afghanistan had to keep itself as a buffer state, better to say as "No Man's Land." The aim in creating "No Man's Land" was to keep Afghanistan in a state of turmoil so that in longer times, both the British as well as Russians can claim their political supremacy over the region.

The British wanted to halt the Tsarist expansion at the Oxus because they suspected growing Russian interest in Afghanistan and the threat to security of India. In 1869 AD, negotiations started between the British and Russia to create a neutral zone in Central Asia and to prevent the annexation of Afghanistan by the former.

In 1872-73 AD, Afghanistan sought British help to settle the Afghan-Iran boundary dispute concerning the supremacy and Russian expansion towards Afghan frontiers. But British authorities could not satisfy Afghan desires and the Amir declared that, "the English look to nothing but their own interests."

Afghanistan was made a victim when Russians penetrated deep inside the territory. The British authorities felt that a more active policy should be followed in Afghanistan and the Afghan problem was viewed in the context of the eastern question. The then Governor-General in India, Lord Lytton supported the reversed policy from conciliation to compulsion. He said, "Afghanistan is a state, too weak and barbarous to remain isolated and wholly uninfluenced between two great military powers (Britain and Russia). It is our policy to cultivate a strong front on our northwestern boundary. We do not covet an inch of (Sher Ali's) territory, we do not desire to diminish its independence. But we cannot allow it to fall under the influence of different powers whose interests are antagonistic to our own."

During second half of the 19th century, threat of Germany in the competition for world markets increased and Russia joined hands with Britain against Germany. But in spreading the sphere of influence in Afghanistan, both Russia and Britain, remained hostile to each other.

By the late 1870s, Russia had occupied Central Asia and was on the borders of Afghanistan. In 1882 AD, Afghanistan asked for British assistance to defend its frontiers from Russian attack. British, who never wanted to come in conflict with Russia, offered regular annual subsidy for the defence of the northwest frontiers of Afghanistan. Russia annexed Merv and Turkmenia to thwart the British from going northwards beyond Afghanistan. In 1884 AD, the Afghan forces marked into the oasis of Panjdeh, inhabited by Turkmens. But the Afghans were defeated by Russian forces. An agreement was concluded between the British and Russia, which was given effect by a protocol signed in London on 10 September 1885, by virtue of which Panjdeh Oasis was recognized as a Russian possession, while Russia handed over Zulfiqar region to Afghanistan. The Afghan boundary question was settled in September 1885, but was reopened only after two years in 1887 AD when Russian annexed Karki and Khwaja Salar. The boundary of the region was demarcated during 1886-88 by an Anglo-Russian mission, not by Russo-Afghan mission, which indicates the pivotal position of Afghanistan. In fact, the failure of the territorial motives of the British expedition to Afghanistan in 1878-80 and the crisis of 1884-85 when Russia occupied Panjdeh, compelled the two imperialist powers, Russia and Britain, to delimit the northern frontiers of Afghanistan. But the northwestern boundaries of Afghanistan had never been properly demarcated to make their grip strong over Afghanistan, British authorities arranged an interview between Amir Abdul Rahman and the Viceroy of India in April 1885 at Rawalpindi, in which it was decided to maintain the integrity of Afghanistan and the Afghan national independence meet the Russia aggression under the immediate influence of the Russian Revolution of 1905-07. A new period in Afghanistan affairs began in 1907 when Russian and British settled their rivalry for the time being. In February 1907, British authorities handed over an outline of the views of the British government regarding an agreement to Russia, without taking any notice of Afghan or Indian viewpoints.

After World War I, Russia and Britain wanted to cooperate with each other and maintain close commercial relations. But they could not wind up their rivalry. This ruined the economic interests of Afghanistan and the two way trade relations with other countries also faded away slowly and steadily. The Afghans had to depend on British India or Russia for their commercial institutions. In this way, Afghanistan could not strengthen itself economically and politically. Its economic as well as political spectrum was disrupted and as such could not prevail upon and consequently was dependent on Russia and other allied powers for its existence. In this way, Russians maintained their politico-economic grip over the territory of Afghanistan.

It can be deduced that presence of Russians in Afghanistan had its political-economic ambitions. They (Russians) had an aim to cover the whole territory, so as to maintain a complete economic and political supremacy within the region as a whole.

REFERENCES

1. Adamee, L. W., *Afghanistan 1900-23*, Los Angles (US), 1967.
2. Ahady, A. H., "The Decline of Pashtun in Afghanistan", *Asian Survey*, 1985.
3. Bellow, H. W., *The Races of Afghanistan*, Calcutta, 1880.
4. Bilgrami, Asghar H., *Afghanistan and British India, 1873-1907: A Study in Foreign Relations*, New Delhi, 1972.
5. Edward S. S., *Russian Projects Against India*, London, 1885.

6. Endin, X. J., *Soviet Russia and East, 1920-27*, California, 1964.
7. Grassmuch, G., *Afghanistan: Some New Approaches*, Ann Arbour (US), 1969.
8. Sen Gupta, Bhabani, *Afghanistan: Politics, Economics and Society*, Frances Pinter Publishers, London, 1986, pp. 10, 15, 16, 21.
9. For Indian view of the struggle over Afghanistan and its significance, see Raja Mohan, C., "US, Iran Jockey for Position in Afghanistan", *The Hindu*, (Weekly edition), 30 August, 1993, p. 13.
10. Ispahani, Mahnaz Z., *Roads and Rivals: The Politics of Access in the Borderlands of Asia*, London, 1989.
11. James, B., *Afghanistan Journey*, London, 1933.
12. Kakar, H., *Afghanistan: A Study in Internal Political Development*, Lahore, 1971.
13. Kakar, Hasan, *Government and Society in Afghanistan*, The University of Texas (US), 1979.
14. Klass, Rosanne, *The Great Game Revisited in Afghanistan*, New York, Freedom House, 1987.
15. Lawrence Ziring, *Buffer states on the Rim of Pashtun*, London, 1987.
16. Ludving, W., *Historical Dictionary of Afghanistan*, Princeton (US), 1980.
17. Wesson, R. G., *Soviet Foreign Policy in Perspective*, USA, 1996.
18. Wheeler, G., *Modern History of Soviet Central Asia*, London, 1964.
19. Ziring, Lawrence, *Iran, Turkey and Afghanistan: A Political Chronology*, Praeger Publishers, New York (US), p. 194.

2

Turmoils in Afghanistan

Afghanistan has been in turmoil for more than twenty years. Afghan War has seven different stages of approximate similarity to 33 months in length, reflecting the pattern of increasing and decreasing intensity respectively (see Table 1 and Table 2). Each of these stages was marked by changes in political strategy and military tactics, and taken together they show a pattern of increasing intensity through stage four, with declining intensity through the subsequent stages. The transformation of the war through its initial five stages represented the efforts of the erstwhile Soviet Union and Afghan Communist regime to develop a strategy in order to defeat the *Mujahideen*, and the ultimate failure to do so. With the defeat of the Najibullah regime in April 1992, the conflict transformed into a sixth stage of conflict, this time between rival *Mujahideen* groups over control of Kabul and the countryside.[1] The emergenc of the Taliban in October 1994 and their defeat in Mazar-i-Sharif in May 1997 marked the seventh stage.

The Afghan War has been one of the bloodiest, deadliest and most persistent conflicts in the second half of the 20th century. Over two million Afghans were killed. Besides this, 15,000 Soviet citizens lost their lives in Afghanistan. Nearly six million Afghans fled to Pakistan and Iran, representing the world's largest single refugee population of the 1980s, while at least two million more Afghans were internally displaced.[2] Thus, over 50 per cent of Afghanistan's indigenous population (estimated at 16-17 million) was either killed, wounded, or made homeless by the war.[2]

The war spread to almost all parts of Afghanistan. Even residents of the government-held urban centres were not safe. The countryside was ravaged, marked by widespread destruction of villages, fields, orchards, and irrigation system. An estimated 30 million mines were left scattered throughout the countryside, most completely unmarked and unmapped.[3] Afghanistan's natural resources, particularly the huge natural gas reserves near Shiberghan, flowed north to the Soviet Union. Afghanistan's economy is still reeling in crisis. The education system and other modernizing sectors of Afghan society were completely disrupted[4] and the struggle for control of the central government obstructed the efforts to improve the situation in Afghanistan, a desperately underdeveloped country attempting to modernize throughout this century, finally caught up to the modern world-in the form of high-technology warfare. The result has been the destruction of the country, society and their culture besides the genocide of the people.

At the time of the communist coup in April 1978, there was no indication that such a devastating war would occur in Afghanistan. The turbulent history of the country had caused the development of traditional patterns of violence that performed specific roles in society. There was no modern tradition for a war of national destruction. Thus, the war that followed grew out of localized low-intensity rebellions into high-intensity war through various stages.[5]

STAGE : I—From Communist Coup to Soviet Invasion (1978-80)

Three major events occurred in the first stage of the Afghan War: *(i)* a coup in April, 1978, which overthrew Mohammad Daud's nationalist regime and installed the fledging Communist Party in power; *(ii)* a rebellion, perhaps more reactionary than loyalist, broke out in summer of 1978 in response to the coup and the new government's radical reform programme; and *(iii)* the Soviets intervened in December 1979 in response to the deteriorating position of the Kabul government as the rebellion intensified and widened.

The Afghan War began with the Communist coup d'etat by officers in the Army and Air Force on 27 April, 1978. The Saur Revoluation developed out of unrest on both the sides of the political spectrum over Daud's policies. The religious traditionalists were unhappy with this modernization and centralization of authority, which threatened virtual autonomy of the villagers. The PDPA resented the steady erosion of its position caused by Daud's distancing from the Soviet Union.[6]

The new government lasted through the summer of 1978. The Communists moved slowly at first, being frequently troubled by intra-party squabbles. In July 1978, after a rapprochment of one year, Khalq and Parcham split again. The first of a series of purges sent Babrak Karmal and other senior Parchamis abroad as special emissaries. Open violence was kept to a minimum, but the independent-minded Afghan villagers ignored various reform programmes promulgated earlier. No effort was made to suppress Islam and the government officials publicly embraced it.

The moderate approach was somewhat successful, but in late October 1978, a series of sweeping reform policies wiped out all previous progress. A symbolic but disastrous move was undertaken with the introduction of the new National Flag in October of the same year with the traditional Islamic green colour being replaced by the communist red colour. It was quickly followed by new policies regarding land reforms, credit reforms, marriages and mandatory education for both the sexes. Young officials were sent to the countryside to implement these reforms.[7]

These reforms struck at the very heart of the socio-economic structure of Afghanistan's rural society. The sudden nationwide introduction and implementation of these reforms with no preliminary pilot programmes gave ideas about their real purpose. The basis of authority in the rural society was the family and the tribe or clan. Implementation of these reforms completely eroded the underpinnings of these bases of authority; consequently, it is hardly surprising that they were so fiercely resisted. When the Khalq regime signed a Friendship Treaty with the USSR in December 1978, it made clear under whose patronage the restructuring of Afghanistan would occur. Thereafter, the rebellion spread rapidly and unremittingly.[8]

By early 1979, most of Afghanistan was in open revolt against the Khalq government. At least 24 of the (then) 28 provinces of the country had suffered violent situation. The rebellion first developed in the Nuristan valleys of Kunar province in the summer of 1978. By the autumn of 1978, widespread resistance occurred in the Tajik northeast and the central Hazara regions. These pockets of early resistance all began among oppressed minorities and were motivated partly due to traditional ethnic hostility.[9]

Although the initial outbreaks of violence occurred among the minorities, the resistance rapidly spread among the Pushtuns, from whom the major resistance groups developed. Most of the leaders split off from Gulbuddin Hekmatyar's Hizb-i-Islami party[10] and acquired the support of local fronts, some of these parties were comparatively loose coalitions than others. Pashtun resistance was motivated by anger and resentment at the policy reforms, abhorrence of the new government's manifest anti-Islamic ideology, and desire for national liberation.[11] By the spring of 1979, nationwide resistance to the Khlaq regime had developed. Without the pre-existing ethnic tensions and ill-timed government reform policies, it is questionable whether the rebellion would have begun so suddenly or spread so vigorously. At large, it did lead inexorably to the Soviet invasion.[11]

In the early spring of 1979, the cities of Afghanistan witnessed war-like situation. In mid-March, 1979, there was a general uprising in Herat, revolts and uprising in other major cities quickly followed.[12] In April of the same year, Afghan Army units led the mutiny in Jalalabad, killing their Soviet advisers and refusing to fight the resistance.[13] Desertion, unwillingness to serve, and attrition reduced the strength of the Afghan Army and by the end of 1980, it had reduced from 80,000 to 30,000.[14]

The Herat uprising was responsible for two major developments: First, on 27 March, 1978, the hardline Hafizullah Amin assumed the Prime Ministership and active control of the government;[15] and second, the Soviets recognized that they must increase their level of involvement in Afghanistan if the PDPA government was to survive. Accordingly, more advisers and weapons poured into Kabul and the Soviets began to prepare for a possible invasion.[16]

During the politburo meeting of 26 November, 1979, the Soviet leadership committed itself to invade Afghanistan. On 17 December, 1979, there was an assassination attempt on Amin's life, possibly with Soviet complicity. In response, Amin and some loyal troops moved to the Darulaman Palace on the outskirts of Kabul.[17] The Soviets, who had hoped to install Babrak Karmal after assisting another internal coup and assassination, were forced to consider another option.

Shortly before the midnight of 24 December 1979, Soviet troops started landing at the Kabul airport, and then at the airbases at

Bagram and Sindh, and the airport at Kandahar. On 27 December, 1979, the Soviets attacked Darulaman Palace. This citadel was overrun after a night of vicious fighting, during which Amin was killed. By 1 January, 1980, the Soviets had nearly 85,000 soldiers in Afghanistan, they controlled the cities and government, and put their puppet Karmal in power. The initial invasion of Afghanistan was a success and the Stage I of the Afghan War was completed with this.

STAGE : II – National Resistance and Soviet Entrenchment (1980-83)

In the immediate aftermath of the Soviet invasion, great uncertainly gripped Afghanistan during which the Soviets became firmly established their control over cities and large towns. International opinion, especially from the United States, was swift and negative. However, except for symbolic gestures (grain embargo, boycott of Moscow Olympics in 1980) little was done. Meanwhile, the nationwide rebellion against the heavy-handed Khalq regime was transformed into a national revolution against the puppet Parcha government and its Soviet supporters.

The second stage of the war is characterized more by the patterns and trends rather than by discrete events of importance.[18] The war itself quickly got intensified. By the spring of 1980, the Soviets had over 100,000 troops in Afghanistan, and throughout the year engaged in heavy fighting in all parts of the country. Combat was particularly fierce around Kabul, Jalalabad, Baglan and Salang Tunnel area. Violent uprisings also occurred in Kandahar, Herat and Jalalabad that even wrested these cities temporarily from government control. Insurgent activities were witnessed everywhere. Soviet efforts to maintain law and order in Nuristan and the Hazarajat were unsuccessful.

A pattern emerged that would characterize the next two stages of the war. The *Mujahideen* unleashed attacks from the mountains, the Soviets responded with offensives up the valleys to relieve pressure on the cities and major roads. The *Mujahideen* gained control of several parts of Herat, Kandahar, and the other cities, especially at night. In late August 1980, the Soviets launched the first of a series of large scale offensives up the Panjshir Valley against the rebel leader Ahmad Shah Masud. But when they withdrew, the *Mujahideen* resumed control. These patterns of conflict intensified in the next two years, as Soviet-Democratic Republic of Afghanistan (DRA) outposts were established along the horseshoe-shaped main road of Afghanistan.[19]

From 1981 onwards, rural Afghanistan (over 75 per cent of the country) was under the control of resistance groups, except during those periods when the Soviet-DRA forces were directly involved. Meanwhile, the regime and Soviets held the cities and a string of military bases and outposts, the construction of which was finished by the end of 1983. During this stage, the Soviets concentrated on establishing their presence throughout the country, particularly in the northern provinces, along the main road, and in the major cities while mounting periodic major operations into guerrilla strongholds. The targeted areas included the Panjshir (six major operations) and other strategic valleys, and the areas around Herat and Mazar-i-Sharif. Soviet-DRA operations tended to fluctuate between combined arms search-and-destroy missions and garrison duty. During this period, the resistance was divided and weak. Most of the combat *Mujahideen* were inept, poorly armed and trained.

The overwhelming firepower of the Soviet forces coupled with their total air superiority introduced the destructive capacity of modern combat to Afghanistan. Village and civilian population was the targets from the beginning of the conflict, as with all guerilla wars, the inability to distinguish the fighters from the usually supportive non-combatants fostered an indiscriminate attitude by the Soviets. In addition to the atrocities and horrors, this situation created refugees, which later became a serious problem.

Refugees had fled Afghanistan since the mid-1970s in small numbers. By the time of the invasion, some 400,000 were already in Pakistan. However, the 'rubbleization' tactics of the Soviets forced the population to flee in large numbers. By the end of Stage II, there were nearly three million refugees in Pakistan and an unknown number (probably more than 1.5 million refugees in Iran). The big surge in refugees occurred in the first two years after the Soviet invasion, when over four million people fled to Pakistan and Iran, while hundreds of thousands became internally displaced. Suddenly, the Afghan refugee population became the largest in the world (by 1990, Pakistan was host to four million internally displaced in Afghanistan). The strategy that produced these refugees was taken directly from the teachings of Mao Tse Tung and produced what Dupree termed "migratory genocide."[20]

A number of political and economic developments also occurred during this stage. A nascent political opposition headquartered in Peshawar, Pakistan, was formed in 1980, but it was characterized by factionalism throughout this period and after. Western support developed slowly because of the widely held belief that the rebels did not have a chance as it became clear that the war would prolong. The US set-up a Central Intelligence Agency (CIA) unit through Pakistan to funnel aid to the resistance rebel leaders.

The Parchamis, having acquired power, engaged sometimes in violent purge of their arch rivals, the Khalqis. Arrests, torture and executions increased among the general population. Soviet Intelligence Agency, the KGB particularly favoured these methods in 1982-83 after the lack of success by the military operations in 1980-81.

The Soviets virtually ran the government after the invasion. Ministers and departments, which had figurehead Afghan leaders, were unable to conduct even routine business without the approval of Soviet advisers. Even Babrak Karmal had little authority for independent decision making.[21] The Soviets provided substantial economic aid ($ 350 million in 1980 alone). They also signed trade agreements providing Afghanistan with a market for its goods (primarily natural gas, which they got at below market prices), and tripled their arms exports to Afghanistan ($ 683 million in 1980).

Finally, a number of steps were taken to prepare Afghanistan for eventual integration into the Soviet sphere. Over 10,000 children were taken to the USSR for "education" programme, some to last as long as ten years. The northern provinces bordering the Soviet Union underwent especially rigorous pacification campaigns. A "concentric circle" strategy was applied to the northern cities, whereby the Soviets tried gradually to take ultimately pacifying the resident population. The Soviets actually annexed the Wakhan Corridor by the fall of 1980. There were reports that Leonid Brezhnev wanted to annex the eight northern provinces, but the Afghan government, particularly the Khalqi faction, strongly resisted the proposal. By the end of Stage II, the "Sovietization" of Afghanistan was well underway.

STAGE : III – Air War, Interdiction and Destabilization (1983-86)

Stage III of the war emerged in 1983, but no distinct event provides a handy reference point to mark its beginning. The primary difference between the second and third stages was strategic, as the Soviets made a significant change in their military goals. In the first year of the Soviet occupation, their priority was to take control of the cities, protect the northern pipeline, keep the major roads open, and broaden the government's base of support. By 1983, the pipeline and road were as secure as they would ever get. The Soviets controlled 15-20 per cent of the country, primarily the cities and major military installations. It was increasingly evident that the government's base of support could not be easily broadened. In late 1983 and early 1984, the Soviets stepped up their counter insurgency campaign. The gradually increasing *Mujahideen* combat could not keep pace with this. The other major change from the second stage was that conditions in the arena of conflict got changed. Much of the population fled. By late 1983, all parts of the country experienced warfare. The major Soviet installations were established. Thus, the next step for the Soviets was to intensify and widen the war and further weaken the support structure of the *Mujhaideen*. To that end, the Soviets shifted to an "air war" in 1983, bombing villages and depopulating rural areas that provided vital support to the *Mujahideen*.

Urban warfare was particularly fierce in 1983, notably in Herat, Kandahar and Mazar-i-Sharif. Over 3,000 Afghans reportedly died in the retaliatory bombing of Herat in April 1983 and Kandahar was also heavily bombed. After six unsuccessful offensives in the Panjshir Valley, the Soviets negotiated a de facto truce with Ahmed Shah Masud. During the summer of that year, the *Mujhadieen* made two major attacks on Kabul. Finally, the *Mujahideen* offensives in Paktia overran small DRA posts at Jali and Khost and the garrison at Uruzgan was besieged. In late December 1983-early January 1984, the Soviets relieved beleaguered Uruzgan.

Although the Soviet air war strategy continued through the year 1984, numerous other large scale offensives were conducted. A guerilla ambush in March 1984 near the Salang Pass prompted concerted effort to crush the resistance in the Panjshir. Panjshir offensive (seventh in row) occurred during April-September 1984 followed by Panjshir offensive no. eight in October-November same year. The valley was largely depopulated and DRA garrisons were left behind.

Herat and Kandahar were the targets of multi-division offensives with heavy air support in June 1984. Herat also saw heavy fighting in July, August, and in other western provinces in November the same year. The Soviets tried to sweep the valleys around Kabul to reduce *Mujahideen* pressure on the capital. They pushed up the Logar and Shomali valleys in July and August 1984, and destroyed the town of Paghman to the west of Kabul in late November the same year. The introduction and use of 107 mm and 122 mm rockets and SA-7 missiles by the *Mujahideen* allowed the resistance group to keep the pressure on, some of their biggest rocket attacks on Kabul accurred in November 1984. Finally, late in the year (1984), the Soviets made efforts to seal the border with Pakistan, particularly in Paktia.[27]

The emphasis on interdiction of *Mujahideen* supply lines increased during 1985, and the Soviets augmented their air war strategy by the increased use of artillery and rocket launchers to achieve "depopulation through firepower." Nonetheless, the better-armed and tactically sound *Mujahideen* groups conducted several larger operations in 1985 and felt strong enough to stand and fight in the war for the first time.

In January-February 1985, the Soviets made an attempt to relieve their besieged garrison at Marikot, on the Pakistani border in Kunar. They were unsuccessful, but a concerted push in May-June 1985succeeded. Another Panjshir based attack cut the Salang Pass highway between Kabul and Kunduz in March and led to the ninth unsuccessful Panjshir offensive in the summer. In an effort to isolate western Afghanistan from Iran, an offensive in the Helmand Valley in June 1985 was launched, which caused widespread destruction. In the summer that year, an offensive was launched in Herat. Attacks on Khost by the rebels in summer led to a Soviet offensive in Paktia during August-September 1985. Violentincidents averaged over 200 per month during 1985 for the first time and 217 incidents occurred in 24 of the 29 provinces of the country including Nimroz and Hazarajat.

The war leaped in intensity as it shifted into the fourth stage. The first four months of 1986 alone averaged 329 incidents in 26 provinces.[31] There were many major engagements or other incidents throughout the country. Increased *Mujahideen* activity was evident in all the northern provinces. A major battle occurred in early April in Paktia, when a Soviet-DRA force attacked and destroyed an important *Mujahideen* cave complex at Zhawar, but this abated *Mujahideen* pressure in the region only temporarily.

To summarize, two important military trends occurred in this third stage of the war: First, although still not united even after the Peshawar parties formed a political alliance in June 1985, *Mujahideen* combat operations improved in part because support to the *Mujahideen* took on meaningful proportions including use of sophisticated weapons like SA-7 and Blowpipe missiles and 107 mm and 12 mm rockets. The Soviet Press reported about the low morale and poor discipline among the Soviet troops in the war-ravaged Afghanistan during this period.

Despite this, the third stage still belonged to the Soviets. Their strategy shifted from consolidation of the cities, highways and north to focus on the eastern provinces. They also made efforts to improve infrastructure in the north. Tactics changed, special operations and air borne units were deployed to interdict *Mujahideen* supply lines. The ruthless use of air power during this period, which intensified the refugee crisis in the war-torn country, was criticized by one and all. The international community came heavily upon Soviet Russia for the crisis in Afghanistan. On the political front, repeated rounds of talks in Geneva occurred during this stage (April and June 1983, November 1983, August 1984, June 1985). Although little progress had been made since the talks began in 1982, some points of contention were gradually being hammered out. In 1985, Mikhail Gorbachev became the new Soviet leader. The resistance remained hopelessly divided and politically ineffective, despite the creation of a unified front by the seven major parties in Peshawar on 16 May 1985. Lack of progress in broadening regime support led the Soviets to remove Karmal and replace him with former KHAD Chief Najibullah on 4 May 1986. This act marked the end of Stage III.

STAGE : IV – Resistance Gains and Soviet Withdrawals (1986-89)

The political and military patterns of the previous two stages were found during the Stage IV. It was apparent by early 1986 that the *Mujahideen* were slowly losing the war. The Soviet combination of refocusing strategic aims and refining new tactics (in particular, the increased reliance on overwhelming air power) was effectively driving the *Mujahideen* off the battlefield. However, the lengthy conflict was also taking a significant toll on Soviet morale and political will to continue. A new paradox emerged. Soviet military superiority, still incomplete in light of *Mujahideen* successes – most small-scale and minor, some spectacular and symbolic – nonetheless had driven the rebels and civilians out of the country and into defensive. On the other hand, the resistance, which throughout the conflict was more capable militarily than politically, appeared to be winning the political competition for Afghanistan. The people of Afghanistan supported the resistance overwhelmingly with a firm international opinion on their side.

The war in Afghanistan continued to intensify in stage IV. Soviet strategy remained built around destruction of the rural areas that supported *Mujahideen* operations. Nonetheless, many ground operations were conducted, particularly in the zone from Kandahar to Bagram, in the provinces bordering Pakistan. There were also increased combat activities in the northern provinces, from Herat to Kunduz. The insertion of small commando units ambushing supply routes continued to pose a formidable challenge to the *Mujahideen* early in this period.

The most notable expansion of the war was the increased violation of Pakistani and Iranian territory by the Soviet forces. The spillover into these countries, especially Pakistan, took several forms such as air strikes, artillery attacks, terrorist attacks, assassinations, sabotage and manipulation of politically-disaffected tribes. These incidents were tripled in 1986 and remained at this higher level of intensity until the Soviet withdrawal in 1989. The purpose of this deliberate widening of the war was to sow the seeds of discontent among the local population and thus to put pressure on the Pakistani government.

During this stage of the war in Afghanistan, the *Mujahideen* improved their strength and capacity as well. *Mujahideen* operations became larger and more complex with increasing number of offensive operations exceeding the scope of ambushes. In October 1986, certain resistance groups were provided sophisticated US-made Stinger missiles, which culminated in a trend of gradual qualitative improvement in their arsenal. The Stinger missile was the most important of the many new weapons used for the first time in a credible air defence. Reports of incredible accuracy of these weapons compelled the Soviet forces to change their hitherto successful air borne strategy. This led to a reduction in their air missions and reluctance among Russian pilots to fly at low altitude. The sense of impunity with which Soviet fighters, bombers, especially the terrifying helicopter gunship had previously operated was replaced with a more effective and pragmatic strategy.

The statistics for the conflict during Stage IV bear out the contention that the war had escalated to a fever pitch. Data indicate a monthly average of 346 incidents in 26 of the 29 provinces in 1986, an increase of 61 per cent over the monthly rate of the last seven months of 1985. Hard evidence for 1988 and 1989 was unavailable, but accounts indicate that the conflict further increased in intensity, peaking in the months just prior to the Soviet withdrawal.

After Mikhail Gorbachev came to power in Soviet Russia in March 1985, Soviet policy toward Afghanistan began to change. Increasing domestic discontent in Soviet Russia over the Afghan War found more open expression in the Soviet press. This may also be attributed to Gorbachev's liberal policy of *Perestroika* and *Glasnost*. Concerned with the state of the Soviet economy and overall relations with the West, Gorbachev began to pressure his generals and the Afghan allies to bring the war to an end.

After becoming President in May 1986, Najibullah quickly moved to broaden his government. He announced a unilateral ceasefire on 15 January, 1987 as a propaganda policy. However, it was ignored by both the sides from the beginning. This was apparent that Najibullah's government would be no more successful to pacify the general populace.

Unfortunately for the *Mujahideen*, the unified front of the Peshawar parties was also a failure. Internecine fighting between different party factions continued, combined with policy differences and petty jealousies among the Peshawar political parties who had formed an alliance. Thus, the resistance was unable to take advantage and erode the political position of the Kabul government.

In 1987, growing Soviet-American rapprochement increased pressure for a decision on Afghanistan. The "shuttle diplomacy" of indirect talks by Diego Cordavez became more intense. Rounds 6-8 of the Geneva talks were held in 1986, 1987 and 1988. This final set of talks ended in an agreement, signed 14 April 1988 calling for a nine-month phase-wise Soviet withdrawal from Afghanistan. The combat operations reached a new level in 1988. The withdrawal of the Soviet forces was completed on 15 February 1989, which marked the end of Stage IV.

STAGE : V – High-Intensity Civil War (1989-92)

The War did not end after the Soviet withdrawal in February 1989, but transformed into a fifth stage. Many observers expected the Kabul regime to rapidly fall and heightened pressure on *Kandahar* in the southwest part of the country. In March 1989, the joint *Mujahideen* offensive initiated to capture Jalalabad was a blunder and failed after three months. But the important part of this offensive was that it witnessed a change in the *Mujahideen* tactics. They moved from guerrilla to conventional warfare. The war continued with its unchanging intensity for the remaining part of 1989 and in 1990 despite the absence of Soviet combat forces.

The *Mujahideen* were unable to defeat Najibullah until April 1992 for two major reasons: First, the Soviets continued to provide their unstinted support to his regime. During a *Mujahideen* attack, the Soviet troops saved Najibullah in an airlift that was as interesting as the Berlin Airlift of 1948-1949. The amount of the assistance in this airlift varied but was believed to be substantial. This assistance included the newly-introduced FROG and SCUD missiles, which augmented the indirect fire capability of the Kabul government against the Stinger missiles used by the *Mujahideen*. Thousands of Soviet technical and military advisers remained in Afghanistan even after the withdrawal, and there were reports of Soviet soldiers masquerading in Afghan uniforms. There was continued Soviet air support from the military bases in Soviet Central Asia.

Hence, combat operations continued to increase, landmines were scattered around the countryside, and there were efforts to undermine Pakistani support for the *Mujahideen*. The Rawalpindi ammunition dump exploded during this period destroying massive CIA – supplied war material. Pakistan's President Zia-ul-Haq, who was the major supporter of the *Mujahideen*, died in an air-crash in August 1988.

The other major reason for the continuation of the Afghan conflict was the ability of the Afghan resistance to mount a credible alternative. The formation of the Afghan Interim Government (AIG) in February 1989 was a failure, doomed by the bickering among the Peshawar party leaders who were its primary participants. The Afghan Shiite minority was excluded from a role in the AIG, as were the major resistance commanders inside Afghanistan. The AIG fell in late 1989, due to internecine violence among the forces of Hekmatyar and Masud.

In Zia ul-Haq's absence, Pakistani support for the *Mujahideen* became uncertain. Western aid was bottled up in Pakistan. More importantly, Pakistan put tremendous pressure on the *Mujahideen* for a victory against the Soviet forces. This pressure pushed the *Mujahideen* into their ill-conceived offensive in Jalalabad in March 1989, where they demonstrated a lack of cohesiveness, which was essential for successful conventional warfare. The *Mujahideen* unleashed severe attacks on Khost, Herat, Kandahar and Kabul during 1990. A military stalemate existed throughout this stage with DRA forces gaining control over the strategic centres. They took advantage of the political divisions among the *Mujahideen* and their inability to shift from guerrilla tactic to conventional warfare.

Najibullah made conciliatory gestures throughout the year after losing the Soviet support. He moved away from communism toward an Islamic nationalist identity by convening a *Loya Jirga* (National Assembly). He replaced the key ministers of his government and changed the name of the PDPA to *Hizb-i-Watan* (Homeland Party). Najibullah made numerous diplomatic trips abroad and floated several peace initiatives, but all included that he remains all in all or share power and all his efforts went in vain when these were rejected by the resistance group commanders.

In 1991, the resistance groups achieved some gains. In March same year, the long siege of Khost ended in a victory for the *Mujahideen* and they immediately tightened their grip on eastern Afghanistan around Gardez. Division within *Mujahideen* rank and file continued to prevent the establishment of a unified alternative to Najibullah. The well established rift between Islamist and traditionalist parties grew deeper. Ethnic-linguistic and religious differences perpetuated. Iran-based resistance organizations and field commanders made demands to be represented in any political settlement. This situation provided the platform for growing rivalry between Saudi Arabia, Iran and Pakistan to have a say in Afghanistan's political future.

Despite the Khost victory and earlier Jalalabad campaign, this stage of the war was characterized more by the events such as the Soviet withdrawal from Afghanistan in 1989 and the struggle for military supremacy on the ground. In May 1991, the United Nations tabled a peace plan that finally offered Afghanistan the possibility of a transition from fighting, violence and bloodshed. More generally, 1989 brought the collapse of Communism in Eastern Europe and 1990 the implementation of widespread economic and political reforms throughout that region and the Soviet Union. Despite the precipitous economic decline that occurred in the USSR during this period, Soviet military and economic assistance to Kabul continued.

In August 1991, a coup attempt against Russian President Mikhail Gorbachev marked the beginning of the end of the USSR and the Najibullah government in Afghanistan as well. In September 1991, the two superpowers, the USA and the USSR, agreed to cut off military assistance to their respective clients in Afghanistan by the beginning of 1992. The Soviet Union also limited economic aid and tightened restrictions on such aid in late 1991. Gorbachev resigned on 25 December 1991 and the Soviet Union broke apart. With the demise of the Soviet Union, the DRA met its obvious end.

STAGE : VI – Mujahideen Victory and National Fragmentation (1992-94)

When Rashid Dostam's northern Uzbek militia rebelled against Najibullah's government in February 1992, the days of the regime were numbered. Najibullah agreed to step aside under the UN sponsored plan which would replace him with a multiparty interim government. Determined not to be cheated out of victory after fourteen years of war, the *Mujahideen* moved to Kabul in April 1992 in a surprisingly bloodless victory. Najibullah was replaced with an Interim Government established on the basis of the April 1992 Peshawar Accord headed by Sibghatullah Mojadidi, who held power in Kabul only for a couple of months. Mojaddidi reluctantly handed over power to Burhanuddin Rabbani, leader of *Jamiat-i-Islami*, whose Interim Government was authorized to rule for four months, or until October 1992. Rabbani announced himself as the President by an assembly dominated by his supporters in late December 1992. His chief arch rival in this power struggle, Gulbuddin Hekmatyar, rejected this government. In March 1993, eight major parties reached an agreement in Islamabad to allow Rabbani to finish an 18-month term of office, and they made Hekmatyar the Prime Minister of the country.

Despite the Islamabad Accord, an acceptable power-sharing arrangement could not be reached as a result of which fierce fighting continued repeatedly between different groups. Since Najibullah's fall in 1992, there was indeed difficulty in making National Coalition Government a reality.

Since the beginning of the post-Najibullah era, the squabbling between power contenders resulted in widespread violence. Since Ahmed Shah Masud and Rashid Dostam's militia initially controlled most of Kabul district, Hekmatyar's forces launched numerous attacks from their bases south of the city in Charasyab since April 1992, until they fled in the face of the first Taliban advance in the city in early 1995. In one of the most ironic twists of the Afghan war, Kabul, which had survived the earlier stages of the war, became a major battleground. As many as 50,000 people were killed and 150,000 wounded there and hundreds of thousands fled the city. Large areas of the city were reduced to rubble due to violence over the last five years. Despite these casualties, much of Afghanistan was peaceful during this stage.

There was little success in forming a national government during this stage. In the summer and autumn of 1993, fighting in Kabul was primarily between the Iranian-backed Shia party *Hizb-i-Wahdat* and the Saudi Arabia-supported fundamentalist Sunni party of Abdul Rasul Sayyaf, *Ittehad-i-Islami*. In January 1994, fierce fighting erupted between Hekmatyar and Massoud's forces yet again around Kabul city. Dostam's army supported Hekmatyar this time in a coup attempt against Rabbani. Fighting, including air attacks, spread to Dostam's bases in Mazar-i-Sharif and continued at a level of intensity that surpassed the Kabul attack of August 1992. Temporary ceasefires in Kabul did not work out and by March 1994, nearly 1,000 people died in the fighting and over 100,000 were made homeless. Despite the UN mediation led by former Tunisian Foreign Minister Mahmoud Mestiri (who was later replaced by German diplomat Norbert Holi in May 1996), no political arrangement could satisfy all the claimants to power in Afghanistan.

The fragmentation deepened in 1994 and so did the frustration of regional power brokers, especially Pakistan, because it prevented that country from realizing its aspirations to trade and influence in Central Asia. Pakistan and Saudi Arabian fundamentalists began to support Afghan religious students in Pakistan known as the Taliban in the summer of 1994. Their arrival on the Afghan stage marks the end of the period of intra-*Mujahideen* civil war and the beginning of another important but violent saga in the Afghan War.

STAGE : VII – Taliban Era (1994-97)

The Taliban first emerged in October 1994, when they initiated action between Kandahar and the city of Quetta in Pakistan to 'rescue' a Central Asia bound trade convoy from Pakistan in between Kandahar and Herat. Presenting themselves as simply religious students who were fed up with the post-communist struggle for power in Kabul between the *Mujahideen* leadership and the lawlessness elsewhere in Afghanistan, the Taliban quickly found support in southwestern part of Afghanistan. Headed by a council of largely unknown Durrani Pashtun religious scholars and students, the Taliban quickly made inroads into central and eastern parts of Afghanistan, bringing an end to the stalemate that had prevailed since 1992. The Taliban asked drug dealers, warlords and militia commanders to surrender or leave, and many did so, perhaps unwilling to fight against religious students. The Taliban also unleashed some successful skirmishes throughout 1995. They captured Spin Boldak in October 1994, Kandahar in November 1994, Lashkargah in January 1995, and then drove towards Kabul and Herat.

By March 1995, the Taliban took control of about one-third of Afghanistan and were on the outskirts of Kabul. They defeated the Shia *Hizb-i-Wahdat* and killed its leader Ali Mazari. They reportedly committed atrocities against some of the *Hizb-i-Wahdat* soldiers. Gulbuddin Hekmatyar evacuated his positions in south of Kabul and fled east before the Taliban advance. But Masud's loyalists drove the Taliban back from the capital Kabul. For the first time since early 1992, it was no longer a city under siege. In April 1992, the Taliban advance towards Herat was stopped and in May 1992, they clashed with Iranian troops in Nimruz. Resuming their drive towards north in late summer, the Taliban captured Herat in September 1995. After gaining control over 50 per cent area of Afghanistan, the Taliban pushed towards Kabul again. Though by November 1995 they captured the city, by the end of the year (1995), Masud drove them back from Kabul once again.

In early 1996, there was mounting pressure on Rabbani to step down, particularly from the Supreme Coordination Council (SCC). Hekmatyar, Mojaddidi, Dostam, and Karim Khalili (the new leader of the *Hizb-i-Wahdat*) were the pioneers of this pressure. In the meantime, when Hekmatyar felt to have lost the unstinted Pakistani support to the Taliban, he moderated his position early in the year, and finally joined the government as Prime Minister in 1996. An anti-Kabul alliance of the other major opposition leaders emerged in the summer. But by August 1996, Hekmatyar and Dostam reached a truce.

In September 1996, the Taliban suddenly took control of Kabul. They first struck to the east of Kabul, taking Jalalabad and then marching against Hekmatyar's forces which gave up with little fighting. Outflanked and uncertain of their support, Rabbani, Masud and Hekmatyar abandoned Kabul and fled towards the north. Throughout the fall and winter of 1996 and the early 1997, the frontlines shifted back and forth 25-70 kilometers north of Kabul as Masud, Dostam and Khalili formed a somewhat shaky Northern Alliance.

Early 1997 saw the Taliban control in south of the Salang Tunnel, the entrance of which Massoud had blown up to prevent Taliban breakthrough into the north. But in February 1997, the Taliban drove forward and captured key towns just at the mouth of the Salang Tunnel (Charikar, Ghorband), which allowed them to turn toward the centre of the country, pushing back Khalili's forces in their drive through the Shibar Pass towards Bamian. During these months, the Taliban were also pushing forward on their northwestern front.

In May 1997, Dostam's most trusted lieutenant Abdul Malik revolted and took over Mazar-i-Sharif with the assistance of Taliban troops, forcing Dostam to flee abroad. Simultaneously, the Taliban pushed forces through the now open Salang Tunnel. After only four days, a popular uprising in Mazar-i-Sharif led to the massacre of the Taliban vanguard there, while Masud suddenly cut the Salang Tunnel again, isolating their eastern forces around Pul-i-Khumri. After briefly holding over 90 per cent of Afghanistan and being poised for final victory, the Taliban had suffered their most significant defeat of the war. This defeat ended Stage VII of the Afghan war. Despite the slaughter and bloodshed in Mazar-i-Sharif, combat continued to decrease in intensity during this stage, as most of the country was peaceful.

STAGE : VII – Beginning of a New Conflict (from 1997 till date)

The situation has remained fluid since the debacle in Mazar-i-Sharif in May 1996. The Pul-i-Khumri garrison retreated to Kunduz, where they took control of the airport. This force counter-attacked the west in October 1997, pushing into the edge of Mazar-i-Sharif before being driven back again in fierce fighting. Meanwhile, Masud advanced towards Kabul in late July 1997, finally halting just outside of artillery range of the city, while Khalili's Hazara fighters pushed the Taliban out of the central highlands and encircled Kabul on the western side. By November 1997, Dostam had returned to capture Mazar-i-Sharif and Malik went into exile. However, Dostam could not enjoy the same level of strength that he did prior to the May coup. By the end of 1997, the Taliban controlled more territory than they did at the year's beginning, but after their summer and fall of losses, the future of Afghanistan remains clouded.

Ethnic and sectarian difference have been deepened by the Taliban success and also, since their slaughter in Mazar-i-Sharif, by their failure. Whatever mandate the Taliban enjoyed in their early days is gone now, in a conflict that is increasingly being drawn along ethnic and religious lines. The ethnic minorities of the central and northern part of Afghanistan did not accept Taliban control over their areas. Largely because of the continuation of supplies to all warring parties by outside powers, both the Taliban and their opponents continue to seek a military solution to the question of who should control Afghanistan and what manner of government the country should have. The foundation for continued conflict increasingly along ethnic lines will characterize Stage VIII.

Despite downward trend in combat intensity in Afghanistan at the beginning of 1998, the ethnic foundations for the continuing violence there make it difficult to predict Stage VIII as one of the stages of the Afghan War. Tragically, this war continued, approaching its twentieth year. For all the devastation that this protracted war often seems to have had, it can be argued that it has progressed through distinct stages. In this chapter, seven major stages of the Afghan War have been identified and examined, revealing a pattern of growing intensity and a propensity to widen into neighbouring countries.

Table - 1
Stage of the Afghan War

Stage	*Date*	*Months*
I.	April 1978 – December 1979	21
II.	January 1980 – March 1983	39
III.	April 1983 – May 1986	36
IV.	May 1986 – February 1989	34
V.	February 1989 – April 1992	38
VI.	April 1992 – January 1994	30
VII.	November 1994 – May 1997	31
VIII.	June 1997 – Present (March 1998)	10

Mean = 32.7 months per stage Standard deviation – 5.7 months.

Range (I.S.D.) = 27.0-38.4 months.

Table–2
Intensity of the Afghan War

Stage	*Intensity*	*Increasing/Decreasing*
I.	Low	Increasing
II.	Med'	Increasing
III.	High	Increasing
IV.	High	Stable
V.	High/Medium	Decreasing
VI.	Medium	Decreasing
VII.	Low	Decreasing
VIII.	Low	Stable

Source: Statistical Indicators for Asia and Pacific, 2000.

Based on the relationship of standard deviation to the mean in a normal distribution, it is deduced that the eighth stage of the war ended in 1999, with about 68 per cent probability of this event failing within ± 5.7 months and a 95 per cent probability of it failing within ± 11.4 months of the date. When the first stage of the war is dropped from the analysis, the mean is 34.7 per stage over the remaining six completed stages, and the standard deviation falls to 3.4 months. This may not be significant if Stage VIII, is also the last stage and, like Stage I, somewhat shorter than the middle stages. To asses the likelihood of that occurrence, consider the pattern of intensity of the war (see Table 2).

Intensity can be assessed in several ways, including number of causalities, frequency of combat and territorial coverage of combat. Considering such determinants, the analysis of the war over the previous stages reveals the following pattern of intensity: From its localized beginnings in Kabul, the war grew in intensity through the 1980s. Combat operations and deaths all mounted and the war was transformed into international conflict that spilled over to neighbouring countries and has far-reaching implications. After the Soviet withdrawal, however, the conflict began to slow down in intensity and much of the country began to have periods of peace and tranquility. However, high intensity combat was witnessed in Kabul. The pattern of intensity over the seven identified stages suggests that Stage VIII could be the last stage of this long and deadly conflict.

At the present juncture, transition from low-intensity conflict to a peaceful atmosphere in Afghanistan is only possible if the lone superpower the United States and other regional powers make necessary efforts. The United Nations and other responsible world bodies should take keen interest to ensure that the present government in Kabul led by Hamid Karzai putting maximum efforts to fulfil the needs of the common people of Afghanistan

REFERENCES

1. Amstutz, *Afghan*istan, 1986 notes the paucity of complete data on the *Afghan* War on p. 130. The monthly *Afghan*istan Report, published by the Institute of Strategic Studies, Islamabad Pakistan.

2 Amstutz, *ibid*; Bradsher, *ibid.*, p. 101.

3 *Ibid.*, p. 132.

4 *Ibid.*, pp. 284-90.

5 *Ibid.*, pp. 180-81; David Isby, *Russia's War in Afghanistan* (London: Osprey Publishing, 1986), p. 1.

6. Bradsher, *ibid.*
7. *Ibid.*, p. 72
8. *Ibid.*, Amstutz, *ibid.*
9. Bradsher, Ibid, p. 85.
10. *Ibid.*, pp. 102-03, 107.
11. *Ibid.*, pp. 163-64, 178.
12. *Ibid.*, pp. 76 and 84.
13. John F. Burn, "Afghans: Now they blame America", *The New York Times Magazine*, 4 February, 1990, p. 27.
14. Louis Dupree, "Post-withdrawal Afghanistan: Light at the End of the Tunnel", in Saikaland Maley (eds.), *The Soviet Withdrawal from Afghanistan*, 1989, p. 30. Also see M.Nazif Shahrani and Robert L. Canfield (eds.), *Revolutions and Rebellions in Afghanistan* (Institute of International Studies, University of California, Berkeley, 1984).
15. Majrooh and S. M.Y. Elmi, *The Socialization of Afghanistan* (Printing Corp. of Frontier Ltd., Peshawar, 1986).
16. Nancy Peabody Newell and Richard S. Newell, *The Struggle for Afghanistan* (Como University Press, New York: Ithaca, 1981), pp. 72-75.
17. *Ibid.*, p. 86.
18. Robert Kaplan, "Afghanistan: Postmortem", *The Atlantic*, April 1989, p. 26.
19. Olivier Roy, *Islam at Resistance in Afghanistan* (Cambridge: Cambridge University Press, 1986), pp. 76-79 and Chapter 7.
20. United States Department of State, "Afghanistan: Eight Years of Soviet Occupation",Washington, Bureau of Public Affairs, *Special Report No 173*, December 1987), pp. 14-17.
21. US Committee for Refugees, *World Refugee Survey, 1988* (Washington, DC: AmericanCouncil for Nationalities Service, 1989), pp. 33-34.

3

Economic Profile of Afghanistan

Any immediate improvement in Afghanistan's economy is hindered by two key factors. First, the continuing drought has prevented any significant improvement in the agricultural sector – the sector upon which around 80 per cent of Afghans are dependent for their livelihood. Second, the poor security situation (particularly outside Kabul) works against investment, such as in irrigation projects that could boost agricultural output. The UN estimates that around 80 per cent of Afghans are living below the poverty threshold of one US dollar a day. The Asian Development Bank (ADB) plans to focus on main priority areas across the country where people are especially vulnerable.[1]

However, programmes have been implemented to step up agricultural economy, reconstruction and rehabilitation. Operations will focus on capacity building, physical infrastructure, rehabilitation process, revitalization of agriculture, rural development, social amelioration, gender empowerment and private sector development. According to World Bank reports, the private sector in future can prove to be an engine of economic growth. During the reconstruction phase, however, the administration is expected to play a leading role while a suitable environment for private sector is created. Once an appropriate legal, financial and security situation is in place, the ADB believes that the private sector may drive progress in the following areas: domestic trade and commerce; external trade; market institution and pricing processes; financial intermediation; agricultural production and marketing; the delivery of services; small-and medium-scale irrigation system development; technology development and dissemination; natural resource management; and mass communication.[2] In this way, there will be an unprecedented use in economic growth and economic policy.

There are no recent accurate data on Gross Domestic Product (GDP). Official statistics has been non-existent since the collapse of the Communist government in 1992. In April 2002, the ADB estimated that the average income per head had fallen to US $ 200 from US $ 300 six months earlier. Despite the problems stemming from drought and security situation, rates of real GDP growth were high in 2002-03. This has partly reflected the low base for comparison-levels of economic activity as the Taliban collapsed. Therefore, an increase in industrial output in 2002 was low, while in 2003 and 2004, it had maintained at least stable growth.

Rates of price inflation, for which there are no data, are likely to be high at the present moment. The drought has lowered food availability and decimated livestock herds. The availability of food aid is also thought to be inadequate. Improved climatic conditions in future would moderate price pressures.

External Sector

Historically, Afghanistan has been facing a trade deficit. Exports are currently minimal. Should the security situation improve, imports are likely to increase rapidly as the reconstruction process is underway. The imminent introduction of a new currency has increased foreign exchange. Given the massive official trade deficit, uncertainty over grant inflows, and the illegal nature of the main export earner, the exchange rate of any new currency is likely to gradually have downward trend over 2002-03.[2]

Economic Policy

Afghan government is still in need of additional international help to deal with its budget deficit, which was forecast to be US $ 257.2 million in 2003-04. Presently, the government's economic policy, which is in fluctuation, is expected to have normal rate of growth after establishment of the provincial governments in which all sectors of economy will be maintaining certain amount of growth and development. Recent estimates reveal that Afghanistan's annual budget is spent on education and expenditure. Present government is in the process of centralizing the collection of tax revenue. Recently, provinces in central Afghanistan have a delivery of more than US $

200,000. However, the trade with the Islamic Republic of Iran and the Central Asian Republic of Turkmenistan has resulted in the boosting up of tax income revenue. It is, of course, a crucial step for the new administrator which can help the government in framing their economic policy.

Banks, which were almost in stagnant position, are now gaining momentum after being revived by new officials. Present government machinery has almost gained public trust in financial institutions. Recent figures reveal that Central Bank is now paying 13 per cent interest on saving accounts. Private sector banks have also been regularized and steps have been taken for privatization of state banks. The central banks in Afghanistan are negotiating with foreign banks for establishment of more new banks across the country.

International Food Aid

UN World Food Programme (WFP) called for increasing donor assistance for Afghanistan. The WFP is currently feeding ten million people in Afghanistan. Currently, ten countries provide 90 per cent of the food distributed in Afghanistan. WFP officials said that less aid would be needed in the months after the July harvest, but that home grown food could run out at shorter span of time. The WFP had helped to prevent a widespread famine by providing sustained aid, which is further needed in times to come for easing poverty and providing jobs to many people.[3]

Government revealed its plans and programmes for re-issuing the Afghan currency. The nominal value would be increased a thousand fold in a bid to establish monetary stability and attract foreign investment. The German Central Bank is providing technical support. An International Monetary Fund (IMF) proposal to use the US dollar as an interim currency in Afghanistan has been dropped. Afghanistan needed its own currency to instil confidence and promote foreign and local investments.[4] Decision of the future of the currency notes issued in Afghanistan would be taken when new currency notes are introduced. Afghanistan Bank sold millions of US dollars to improve the Afghan economy.

Domestic Economy

Government administrations in Afghanistan are coordinating with foreign companies to invest in Afghanistan as a means to encourage foreign investment. Explaining that the government had other priorities (security, law and order) during its first six months in office, Afghan President Hamid Karzai promised that corruption and bureaucracy, which have hampered the business ambitions of returning Afghans, would soon be tackled. The main aim was to encourage businessmen to come up with measures that they thought would bring in private investment.[5] Government is committed to establish an absolutely transparent investment environment in order to save the government and country from economic crisis.

Health Priorities

World Health Organization (WHO) estimated that majority of people in Afghanistan were suffering from cholera and diarrhoea. In response, the new government has launched public health campaigns on cleanliness and hygiene. According to a survey, which began in remote areas in 2002, outbreak of such epidemics has continued throughout the year 2003. Malnutrition and poor healthcare have made many Afghans vulnerable to these deadly diseases. According to WHO, Afghanistan has one of the world's worst health outlooks, with basic healthcare services unavailable to around one-quarter of the population. The WHO estimates that two billion US dollars are needed to provide minimal health care over the next ten years.[6]

Healthcare strategy has been formulated involving representations from each province of Afghanistan as well as from each UN agency for implementation of better health care centres. Following four priorities were identified:

- Control of infectious diseases, including the vaccination of more children and an upgrading of the knowledge and skills of healthcare workers;
- Ensuring that Afghan women, who currently have one of the world's highest maternal mortality rates, have healthy reproductive lives;
- Improving nutrition for all Afghans (according to UN figures, 50 per cent of children are malnourished); and
- Addressing the country's mental health crisis. The WHO estimates that 40 per cent of the population is suffering from psycho-social problems; other studies say that post-

traumatic stress, disorder and other war-related conditions affect up to 80 per cent.[7]

The UN Children's Fund (UNICEF) said in July 2002 that there had been a massive return of Afghan children to schools across the country since they reopened following the fall of the Taliban. About 30 per cent of school children were female. However, in the southern part of the country (the former Taliban stronghold), only 10 per cent of students were female. The survey conducted by the UN and the Afghan Ministry of Education said that nearly 1.25 million children had returned to school in the 20 provinces covered so far. The UN Educational, Scientific and Cultural Organization (UNESCO) appealed for US $ 27 million to meet an urgent need for school supplies, facilities and training. The organization plans to focus efforts on rehabilitating Kabul University, training educated professionals and developing non-formal and distance learning programmes to tackle one of the world's highest illiteracy rates, estimated at 64 per cent. According to UNESCO, over the past 20 years Afghanistan has lost an estimated 200,000 education experts and academics, and 17 universities were devastated.[8] The US Ambassador to Afghanistan provided the Ministry with internet connections and ten computer terminals to help Afghan businessmen to communicate worldwide. UNESCO has set up a Computer Training Centre and an Internet Service in the Journalism Faculty of Kabul University.

Although the industrial area of Kabul is ruined, factories are beginning to return to life. The raisin cleaning factory, a family-run business that provides jobs to 70 workers, annually exports around 4,000 tonnes of raisins to Russia and 1,000 tonnes to the UK, making an annual profit of US $ 40,000-45,000 per year has now started gaining momentum. Gulabudin Sherzaye once ran a multi-million dollar business before he was jailed and his assets seized. Since his release from jail after the fall of the Taliban, Sherzaye has pledged to make a comeback and is trying to reclaim his wide property portfolio in Kabul as well as the seized assets. Afghan entrepreneurs have launched famous Afghan Wireless Communication Company (AWCC) with the help of their Western partners and are planning for much more in future.[9]

Countries like Russia began a new phase of humanitarian aid programme to Afghanistan when it started delivering thousands of tons of supplies - mainly food, blankets and clothes. Japan approved three million US dollar emergency aid at the end of June 2002. The Afghan government planned to channel this aid through the UN Development Programme (UNDP). The funds will be used to expand a job-creation programme that has been underway in Kabul and Kandahar.

The World Bank Projects

The World Bank planned three development projects in Afghanistan, which aim creating jobs in rural areas for groups including ex-combatants and those returning home, either from abroad or from elsewhere within Afghanistan. Grants are also being given directly to the communities for small rehabilitation works and the development of community assets with an aim of kick starting economic activity. Further infrastructure facilities for rapid reconstruction programmes have been made possible, which will reinstate urgently needed water and sanitation supplies in secondary cities, including capital Kabul. The projects will also generate short-term employment. The Emergency Education Rehabilitation and Development Project is focusing on area not covered by other donors. This includes a countrywide plan for learning and skill development and support for the rehabilitation of universities and colleges, education policy and the establishment of a Distance Learning Centre. According to the annual food assessment of the Food and Agriculture Organisation (FAO) and the UN World Food Programme (WFP), agricultural production in 2003 was 52 per cent higher than in 2001-02, but is still 800,000 tons below the average production in 1999. The rise was attributed to relatively better rainfall, and higher quality of seed, fertilizers and other inputs. However, it is still estimated that a huge economic budget is needed in order to rehabilitate the agricultural sector.[10]

The FAO and WFP assessment also found that livestock numbers have fallen by up to 60 per cent owing to the effect of drought on vegetation and the availability of seeds, particularly in non-irrigated areas. These developments have badly affected the Kuchi population, which has a nomadic and livestock-tending lifestyle. This, in turn, has affected other Afghans who depend on the Kuchis for the supply of meat. Severe drought is still found in southern and eastern parts of Afghanistan. The water table is too low to meet the normal demand. This is likely to encourage a population shift to urban areas. Despite

Afghanistan's inability to produce enough food to feed its population, poppy production recovered 3,400 tonnes in 2003 after falling below 200 tonnes in 2002. The increase has occurred despite a decline in arable land in the past decade. However, experts are apprehending that Afghanistan will descend into lawlessness and violence unless donor nations provide aid.

Planners of the country have an assessment for highways, dams and power sector. The World Bank has said that road construction is a priority and the US, Japan and Saudi Arabia have jointly promised to build roads linking Kabul with the main trading cities in the south and west and Kandahar. Afghan authorities have argued that the need for emergency aid will not end until the causes of poverty are addressed. They also appealed the donor countries to give assistance directly to the government[11] rather than through the UN agencies. The Finance Minister elaborated that the priority projects as national solidarity, emergency public works, education and urban infrastructure, water resource management, national governance infrastructure and transport and communication. He said that the government and aid agencies had promised full accountability regarding the use of the US aid. Present budgeted funds were insufficient for construction. It is further deduced that economic policy of the country will prove successful in case all financial assistance come directly to the Afghan government and should not fall at the hands of the UN agencies. That is why economic growth and economic policy may maintain frequency momentum.[12]

More than 600 Companies have been given permission to operate in Afghanistan and these large scale programmes are a step towards better growth in economic structure and economic reconstruction. However, the US has provided them short term loans and planners of the country are aiming at long-term economic reconstruction policy. It is hoped that other donor countries are also trying to invest in Afghanistan. New currency has also forwarded economic policy and has raised confidence in the flow of money market. The issuing of new currency is also an important political step for the Afghan government.[13]

Meanwhile, disgruntled traders in southern Afghanistan found a temporary solution to the disagreement over customs levies when the Governor of Kandahar agreed that duties should be paid only in the region where the traders are registered. Until then traders often had to pay double duties and the southern authorities had also increased the levies due on imported goods. As a result, some traders had stopped declaring goods. Traders also agreed to Governor's suggestion that they open a liaison office in the Kandahar Customs Office. The agreements were set to be re-negotiated following the introduction of the new currency.[14]

UN Food Aid Efforts

The UN along with other international donors has sanctioned aid to ensure that millions of Afghans get enough food in times to come. The funds would be used to make up a shortfall of 84,500 tons of cereal to help refugees and internally displaced people as well as people residing in remote areas. The Aid Programme will focus on the north, west, southern provinces of Kandahar and Central highland areas, where winters are particularly harsh. According to the UN, most of these are displaced ethnic Pashtuns and the main concern is that these groups do not suffer further displacement. International donors under the leadership of the UN are stepping up their aid programme to provide shelter for Afghan returnees. They have hoped to build 40,000 housing units, mostly in central Afghanistan, to house around 300,000 Afghans. It is estimated that around 40 per cent of returnees-approximately 980,000 people are in dire need of shelter. Other aid agencies are also construing shelters in coordination with the Afghan government. The UN Habitat Programme is building 3,000 shelters for 21,000 people in the north of Kabul. The agency has also helped people there to set up local workshops enabling craftsmen to buy material and employ apprentices.[15]

The International Red Cross Committee (ICRC) launched a three-to five-year anti-parasite veterinary programme in order to tackle the diseases attacking Afghanistan's already decimated livestock. The programme concentrates on the provinces of Mazar-i-Sharif, Ghor and Bamian. The ICRC hopes to treat around 5,000,000 animals in 2006. Afghan farmers depend on animals for traction power during planting and harvesting as well as for fertilizer, fuel, milk, meat and wool. The ICRC says that its programme is intended to boost meat production by three kgs per sheep and goat and by up to eight kgs per cow. Given present numbers of the livestock, this would increase the total meat production to 75,000kg.[16]

The Domestic Economy

Top priority for the government is to establish basic infrastructure in rural areas to ease pressure on urban areas so that Kabul and even surrounding areas can absorb more refugees. Almost two million refugees had returned to Afghanistan, the largest single refugee repatriation in 30 years. Since March 2003, more than 1.5 million refugees have returned from Pakistan and since April 2003, around 300,000 have returned from Iran.[17] The remaining returnees are from Central Asia. Rates have now dropped to around 4,000 per day, from a peak of 20,000 per day in May 2003. In early October 2003, the UN Refugee Agency (UNHCR) said that many recently returned refugees, including at least 215 families in just one week, have left again, owing to fears over security.

The Asian Development Bank (ADB) approved grants to repair parts of the road between Kandahar and the border peripheral areas. It is estimated that the project will provide jobs for 10,000 refuges and internally displaced people (IDPs). The ADB says that the focus on returnees and IDPs is to alleviate pressure on Kabul, and that at least 200,000 people have settled temporarily around Kandahar. The Public Works Ministry is carrying out the road construction scheme. The ADB agreed a four million US dollars grant to help rebuilding the formal education system and providing non-formal education for street children, former child combatants and ex-soldiers. About 750 teachers will get refresher training and about 1,000 construction jobs will be created. The grants for both these projects have come from the Japan Fund for Poverty Reduction (JFPR), financed by Japanese government.[18]

According to the preliminary findings of the UN Environment Programme (UNEP), some areas in Afghanistan will be unable to support human life. Groundwater levels have dropped significantly and groundwater itself is turning salty, partly as a result of erosion; drinking water wells were rapidly draining the groundwater and the waste management in urban areas was practically non-existent and every aspect of the environment had been damaged by the combination of conflict and drought.[19]

UN Food and Agricultural Organization (FAO) campaign had been relatively successful in controlling a locust outbreak in northern Afghanistan. The FAO estimated losses by seven per cent in the three most seriously affected provinces, which were also the country's most productive agricultural areas – Baghlan, Samangan and Kunduz. According to the UN, the locusts had jeopardized 70 per cent of crop production in northern Afghanistan.

Drugs Production and Trade

Afghan government had failed to eradicate opium poppy production. The Drug Control and Crime Prevention (ODCCP) estimated that production in 2003 was 3,400 tonnes. In the late 1990s, Afghanistan was the world's largest opium producer, supplying 70 per cent of general supply, and 90 per cent of the heroin in Europe. The Taliban banned opium production in 2000 and this largely stopped cultivation in 2001. The new Afghan government issued a similar decree in early 2002, but by then most crops had already been planted and farmers were reluctant to give up their lucrative yield.[20]

The resurgence of Afghan opium production was also encouraged by the heroin shortage caused by the absence of the usual spring harvest in 2001. The subsequent depletion of accumulated stocks pushed opium prices up ten times, creating a powerful incentive for Afghan farmers to plant poppy in 2001 for the 2002 harvest. In its 2002 Afghanistan opium survey, the ODCCP said that almost 95 per cent of cultivation took place in five of the country's 32 provinces, although poppy was grown in 24 provinces. The report estimated that cultivation took place in over 74,000 hectares. The average opium yield is estimated at 46 kgs per hectare, compared to 24 kgs in 2001. The agency said that the increase was a result of the resumption of cultivation on irrigated land in southern and eastern Afghanistan and more favourable climatic conditions.[21]

The ODCCP said that the domestic price of opium recently fluctuated. Between 1994-2000, prices fell as low as US $ 300/kg and, in early 2001, to US $ 700/kg. After the 11 September 2001 terrorist attacks, the price fell to US $ 350/kg. With the current high price of opium, the total income for Afghan poppy farmers' could surpass one billion US dollar, which would be a record. According to the ODCCP assuming average poppy cultivation of 0.3 ha per farmer, the average income in 2002 could be a few thousand dollars. Previously, average income ranged from US $ 400-600. The opium production had gone high in the south followed by the eastern provinces and Kandahar in the south. According to the UN Special

Envoy to Afghanistan, poppy growing is 40 times more profitable than growing wheat. However, at present government is keen to find out other alternatives. Planners are looking forward for bringing more opium land under grain cultivation. They are trying to do so with the intention to enrich agricultural sector. The ODCCP is working on a pilot project in Kandahar and Badakshan that has involved in giving farmers a small amount of money in return for growing crops other than poppy.[22]

In collaboration with power communication system of Uzbekistan, electricity supply connections have been made possible in border areas. Experts are trying for more feasibility connections in central and south eastern parts of the country, UN Development programme have made mobile connections possible in almost all parts of the country. Power based industries are now working in Afghanistan. Indian government granted Airbus aircraft to the national carrier Ariana Afghan Airlines, and it plans to hand over another two Airbus planes. On 25 September, Ariana Afghan Airlines began direct flights between Frankfurt and Kabul via Istanbul and Sharjah. This is the only scheduled service from Kabul airport. In August, Peruvian engineers installed the equipment and repaired Ariana's planes.[23]

A US-based Human Rights group (PHR) released a report that the maternal death rate was 593 per 100,000 live births, the rate being worse in rural areas. According to PHR, this places Afghanistan higher than every country apart from Sierra Leone. One of the reasons attributed for the high rate was an unwillingness to go to hospital either for cultural reasons or owing to an inability to pay transport costs. According to UNICEF, complications during pregnancy or birth are responsible for 42 per cent of the deaths of women aged between 15 to 45.[24]

Foreign Trade and Payments

The Afghan government announced that it would temporarily reduce customs tariffs on exports in order to boost trade. The Finance Minister held talks with his counterparts and other leaders of several countries, including the US, in his bid to increase Afghanistan's exports. Currently, most of the country's tiny export trade is with Pakistan and Iran and consists primarily of carpets, dried fruits, sheep skins and precious stones. Although many untapped mineral and energy resources could be exploited, the government's immediate concern is to regain control of the country's huge trade in imported goods from warlords, who control the main access routes to Afghanistan.[25]

The Asian Development Bank (ADB) provided grant loan assistance and multi sector programme loans, focusing on governance, transport, energy and the finance sectors. The financial assistance can also help for emergency infrastructure rehabilitation and reconstruction, concentrating on large-scale irrigation schemes, roads, petroleum storage and civil aviation facilities.[26] The ADB is also working with the Public Works Ministry to find out the possibilities of building several major roads, including Pul-e-Khumri via Mazar-i-Sharif and Shiberghan to Khani Chahar Bagh; Kabul to Bamiyan; Kabul via Gardez to Khost; and Kabul to Jalalabad. Feasibility studies are being carried out to asses the roads in central and northern Afghanistan and the reconstruction needs of airports and dams. In addition, the ADB has earmarked funds for technical assistance to look at critical transport concerns and is providing assistance for education, health, community and social mobilization schemes. The US, Japan and Saudi Arabia announced a joint effort to help rebuild the 600-mile long Kabul Highway from Kandahar to Herat.

Other Aid Efforts

The Economic Cooperation Organization (ECO), which comprises Iran, Pakistan and Turkey as well as Azerbaijan, Kazakhstan, Kyrgyzstan, Tajikistan, Turkmenistan and Uzbekistan set up a fund to help rebuild the war-ravaged Afghanistan. The ECO team is making rapid progress in the construction of a trans-Afghan pipeline to carry gas from Turkmenistan to Pakistan. Iran supported construction projects in Afghanistan and provided scholarships for Afghan students. Iran government also issued permission for Iranian traders to continue "export barter business" with Afghanistan due to which Iranian export traders have increased their exports to Afghanistan.

Along with this, Indian administrators and planners opened transit points on the borders of Afghanistan that has made business prospects more feasible. Indian Ministry of External Affairs (MEA) has provided aid to Afghanistan. India has extended help by training diplomats, doctors, teachers and police. Besides, a large number of Indian companies are looking ahead for investment in Afghanistan. During a four-day "Made in India" exhibition, more than 200 Indian companies participated.[27]

The joint Economic Commission between Pakistan and Afghanistan was reestablished after a ten-year gap, following a meeting between Afghan authorities and Pakistani Prime Minister, Shaukat Aziz. They discussed the Afghan Transit Trade Agreement and Pakistan's help in the establishment of banks, post offices and micro-credit facilities in Afghanistan. Pakistan gave the proposal to spend some portion of this aid to reconstruct the Kabul-Jalalabad road. By building this road, both the countries could benefit from bilateral trade and trade with Central Asia. Pakistan and Afghanistan could also link Central Asia, the Middle East and European countries.

The China National Electric Equipment Corporation (CNEEC) opened an office in Kabul in late August 2002, making it the first Chinese company to do so since the civil war began. The CNEEC is reconstructing an irrigation project in Parowan province, north of Kabul. The Chinese Ambassador to Afghanistan said that the Parowan project is the first step towards Chinese efforts in Afghanistan reconstruction, and China also is looking forward to greater economic and trade ties.[28] Thus commendable efforts have been made by the international community for the Afghan reconstruction.

REFERENCES

1. "Excerpts from the Memoirs of Zeki Velidi Togan", in H. B. Paksoy (ed.), *TheRediscovery of History* (New York; M. E. Sharpe, 1994).
2. Ahmed Rashid, *The Resurgence of Central Asia. Islam or Nationalism*? (London: Zed Books, 1994).
3. Shirin Akiner, "The Kazakh Republic, Regional Surveys of the World", *The Far Eastand Australasia* (Londres: Europa Publication, 1992), pp. 1004-05.
4. Barnett, R. Rubin, *The Fragmentation of Afghanistan: State Formation and Collapse in the International System* (New Haven: Yale University Press, 1995), p. 65.
5. Beverley Male, *Revolutionary Afghanistan* (New York: St Martin's Press, 1982).

6. Bess Brown, "Three Central Asian States form Economic Union", *Research Report*, Vol. 3, No. 13, 1 April, 1994.
7. *Central Asia Monitor*, No. 1, 1994, US.
8. *Central Asian Survey*, Vol. 13, No. 1, 1994, London.
9. Central Intelligence Agency, *World Facts Afghanistan*, 2001, www.cia.gov.
10. A. S. Giridharadas, *Afghanistan and 9/11*, Roli Books, New Delhi, 2002.
11. Hafizullah Emadi, *Politics of Development and Women in Afghanistan* (New York: Paragon House Publishers, 1993).
12. IMF, World Bank, and Organization for Economic Co-operation and Development, A Study of erstwhile Soviet Economies, US, 2000.
13. G. Kish, *Economic Atlas of Soviet Union*, US, 1960.
14. Louis Dupree, *Afghanistan*, Princeton: Princeton University Press, 1973), p. 504.
15. P. E. Lydolph, *Geography of USSR*, Willes, 1977.
16. Charles M. Macgregor, *Central Asia Part VI*, Foreign Department Press, 1873.
17. W. Maley, *United Nations and Afghanistan*, New York, New York University Press, 1997.
18. Sheila Marnie and Whitlock, "Central Asia and Economic Integration", *RFE/RL Research Report*, Vol. 2, No. 14, 2 April, 1993, pp. 34-44.
19. Martin McCauley, "Agriculture in Central Asian and Kazakhstan in the 1980s", in ShirinAkiner, *Political and Economic Trends in Central Asia*, Londres, 1994.
20. R. Millor, *Erstwhile Soviet Union and its Geographical Problems*, London, 1982.
21. Ahmed Rashid, *ibid.*
22. Sazman-e-Tadaruk Bara-e-Eijadi Hizbi Kamunist Dar Afghanistan (Akhgar) Afghanistan (Tehran: n.p., 1980).
23. Boris Rumer, "Central Asia's Cotton Economy and its Costs", William Fierman, *Soviet Central Asia: The Failed Transformation*, 1991.
24. *Sazman-e-Tadaruk Bara-e-Eijadi Hizbi Kamunist Dar Afghanistan*, ibid.
25. Seminar on NGOs and Civil Society (UNDP: Tashkent, 1994), p. 48.

26. *Statistical Indicators for Asian and Pacific*, 1994-2000, US.
27. World Bank, *World Development Report*, (Washington: Oxford University Press, 1995).
28. World Trade Organization, *The Results of the Uruguay Round of Multi-lateral Trade Negotiations, The Legal Texts* (Geneva, 1995).

4

Afghanistan as a Nation State

Afghanistan, with its complex ethnography of Afghans, Tajiks Hindukush Indo-Aryans, Turko-Mongolians, strong tribal affiliations, still locked in, what Ibn-Khaldun called, "the first or second stage of civilization", is still in the throes of transformation towards a modern nation-state. Democracy and nationalism have never penetrated roots in this country. The participation of so many international actors, domestic strife and civil wears and a host of anthropological factors contribute to the sorry state of affairs in this country.

Estimates of the proportion of ethnic groups (based on language and sectarian affiliations) in Afghanistan are highly contested and increasingly politicized. Early 1970's estimates gave following estimates: Pashtuns, 47 per cent; Tajiks-Farsiwans-Aiwaqs 34; Uzbeks, Turkmens and Kirghizs eight per cent; Hazaras, seven per cent, Balochs-Barahuis, 2.5 per cent and other Muslim and non-Muslim groups, including Hindus, Sikhs and Jews 0.5 per cent. Based on 1970 estimates, Sunnis constitute 88 per cent and the Shias 12 per cent of the Muslim population. Jonas Hanaqay, a European scholar on Afghanistan says that Abdali tribe embraced Islam towards the end of the 9th century and the remainders of the Afghan people followed their footsteps later. Historically, Muslim Arab armies penetrated the region at the turn of the 8th century AD and the process of Islamization continued gradually. The province of Kabul resisted conversion to Islam much longer than other eastern provinces, and it was only under the Ghznavids that this was fully achieved.[1]

Many Muslim empires rosé in the area during the following centuries and expanded the frontiers of the then Muslim world into Central and South Asia. Modern Afghanistan is the remnant of one of the last such great Muslim empires in the region, the Durrani empire founded by Ahmad Shah Durrani (1747-1772 AD). The Durrani empire began to disintegrate at the turn of the 9th century owing to bloody struggles over succession as well as growing external military and political pressures. The prolonged factional wars (1800-1880 AD) encouraged British and Russian colonial encroachment, resulting in two Anglo-Afghan wars (1839-42 and 1879-1880) and considerable territorial losses. The civil wars and colonial intervention left powerful legacies, notably the increasing economic, military and technological dependence of Afghan government of colonial and post-colonial European powers. It has been the policy to keep Afghanistan always in a struggling state. Russian efforts to maintain supremacy over the whole territory of Central Asia had resulted in several bloody attacks on Afghanistan. Afghan rulers could not unite the provincial leaders and failed to maintain peace in the country.

The effects of foreign assistance and intervention began immediately after the second Anglo-Afghan war, when Britain installed Amir Abdur Rehman Khan (1880-1901), a member of the Muhammadzai branch of Durranis. With substantial annual subsidies and technical assistance, Amir Abdur Rehman Khan consolidated power over the entire country. Unlike his predecessors, Amir Abdur Rehman believed that his power as Amir emanated directly from God rather than the support of the people or tribal Khans. He attempted to safeguard the country from internal subversions and external aggressions. He forcibly converted the population of Kafiristan (a province of Afghanistan), the only remaining indigenous non-Muslims in the country, and renamed the province as Nuristan in an attempt to pacify the recalcitrant Hazara Shias of Central Afghanistan.[2]

Amir Ahmed Rehman Khan justified his cruel policies under the garb of Islam. As the head of the state, Amir claimed to be the sole interpreter of religious doctrine and proclaimed that "whether just or despotic, the king must be obeyed", and issued commands such as "don't violate the Muslim law." He rigorously articulated and effectively utilized the main operative principles of Afghan political culture, ideals of kingship, kinship and Islam, buttressed by partron-client and patrimonial practices and by policies of fear and favour. During his reign covering the last twenty years of the 19th century, the Amir gave himself the task of modernizing the Afghan state and nation building. For Afghanistan, the Amir didn't think of a federal system, nor of a pluralistic emporium like the Ottoman *Millat* system, which was in decline at that time. His was not a neo-feudal regime, nor did he allow any possible autonomy for the diverse regions or populations of the Emirate. He crushed his opponents and critics of his programme without pity. He described Hazaras, Kafirs, Ghilzai's inhabitants of northwestern and northeastern part of Afghanistan not as non-Pashtun ethnic groups, but as enemies of the Afghan state.[3] He weakened the pervasive role of *Ulema* and Sufi leaders in the management of Islamic education of *Waqf* (Muslim endowments), setting up of *Shariat* courts, publication of books, Sermons and guidelines for preaching; all these activities were taken up by the state apparatus. Amir's policies remained unchanged even during the reign of his son, Amir Habibullah (1901-19).

Modern nation state, however, seems to emerge in its true sense only towards the introduction of modern schools and the press, new ideas such as constitutionalism, nationalism, liberal secularism, reformism and Islamic modernism, both to complement and to compete with traditional ideas of kingship and kinship. Besides, the Afghanistan authorities have to understand the philosophy of Islam, which is, of course, a basic step towards modern state. Islam, in absolute terms, is creation of a peaceful religion and a message of unifying people of the world under one umbrella. But Afghan rulers and different sectors in the country have not been able so far to understand the message of Islam in its true perspectives due to which, there has always been turmoil in Afghanistan.

Amanullah, the grandson of the Iron Amir and a supporter of modernist nationalist thought, introduced the first constitution of Afghanistan. He attempted to promote the idea of equality and the development of national ideology based on traits common to all citizens of Afghanistan, but he failed.[4] His rule was challenged by a popular armed rebellion supported by some *Ulemas*, dignitaries after which he was forced to exile. His own weakness was that he didn't understand fully the conflict of tradition and modernity in Muslim society. Any attempt to deal with the very theme of identity involves the danger as if the collective or individual identity were there once and for all, in a definite form. The issue of Muslim identity in the modern age is due to diverse responses such as "modernism", "inner radicalism" and some confusing notions such as Islamizing modernity and modernizing Islam. Conceptual confusions and operational anomalies with regard to this issue led ultimately to Amanullah's failure. Very recent failure of Taliban may be attributed to the same cause. Amanullah's reformist programme lacked proper contexts of both history and Islam and contemporary realities. Russian strategy in Afghanistan failed also due to this reason.

Muhammad Nadir Shah (ruled from 1929-33), who succeeded Amanullah, attempted to legitimize his own dynastic rule by constitutional means. He called a Grand Assembly (*Loya Jirga*) of the tribal elders, religious dignitaries and local aristocrats to ratify a new constitution. Islam was once again given the prominent role in society. Discrimination against non-Pashtuns became rampant in the allocation of economic, educational and developmental resources.[5]

The Musahiban rulers (who ruled from 1929 to 1978) pursued ambivalent policies towards Islam, especially in expanding modern educational system, which has a secular agenda and a Pashtun based nationalism. So called modernization programmes in the form of "new democracy" turned out to be mere stage rehearsals. Rulers tried to appease foreign patrons mainly Russia and India throughout the rule of Musahiban. Ties with Pakistan were relegated to the background but was promoted with India, turning a blind eye to the ground reality of Hindu-Muslim, communal divide. Musahiban rulers tried to incite the fellow Pashtuns/Pakhtuns living across the Durand Line against the central authorities of Pakistan. This ultimately proved very costly for the failure of the state of Afghanistan. All the subsequent ideological movements in the country such as communist and Muslim movements always got divided on ethnic/sectarian lines; Tajiks, Uzbeks and Hazaras. It reached a point, where even the geographical integrity of the country was compromised during the post-Soviet era, *Mujahideen* and the Taliban rule.[6]

Promulgation of the liberal constitution of 1964 paved the way for the Marxist and Maoist parties to emerge and in response, Islamic movements too were formed who challenged also Maoist monarchy. In 1966, Professor George Debits, a Soviet physical-anthropologist, made a preliminary draft for a Conference on "The Formation of the Afghan Nation." It suggested a nine-chapter programme, fundamentally historical. It reflected the Soviet theory of socio-economic evolution from individual to tribe, from ethnic group to nationality to nation and state. Soon the Afghan conflict shattered the old certainties on state and nation determinism-national awareness, the development process of national identity as well as the common political future went into crises. July 1973 saw Prince Daud's coup and abolition of monarchy and pro-Soviet policies. Daud, the first President of the Afghan Republic (1973-78), tried to promote the concept of a Pashtun state, which would have the ethnic, cultural and linguistic foundation and legitimacy of Afghan unity. Daud, for instance, prohibited the use of ethnic surnames and ethnonyms. In 1978, Daud himself fell victim to a coup led by the People's Democratic Party of Afghanistan (PDPA) that ended the Durrani dynastic rule[7] by establishing a communist government (from 1978 to 1992). The Kabul communist regime in the 1980's made official the existence of eight nationalities based on the Soviet model, the question of the disparate character of the nationalities or ethnic groups wasn't solved by this policy. Neither the ethnographic maps nor the lists made out by the anthropologists nor the political discourse about nationalities were able to express the complex relationship between Afghan heterogenity and Afghan unity. The *Jihad* against the communist government, which was supported by Pakistan, culminated in the triumph of *Mujahideen*. However, factional struggles continued leading to the emergence of the Taliban. Post-Cold War American tactics are to be deciphered in this scenario. Backfiring of the Taliban experiment for America led ultimately to the establishment of the Hamid Karzai led coalition government. The condition under the Pashtun leader is fluid and real power seems to lie in the hands of Tajik ministers, who were warlords and commanders having a legacy of indiscipline and unfaithfulness more than in the Pashtuns.[8]

Recent attack on the US World Trade Tower has again pushed Afghanistan deep into dark historical period. The presence of US forces in Afghanistan is a hope towards bringing a democratic set up in Afghanistan. Other disintegrating forces are the groups/parties, which have always segregated Afghanistan and will continue to do so in future. All these major fractions have not understood the philosophy of Islam and as such, have destroyed Afghanistan at different stages of history. These fractions are working on the principles of Wahabi school of thought implemented from Najdi Saudi Arabia. Islam has not been understood by these Wahabi Najdi groups. Islam, in its true sense, was practiced and preached by Sufis only. All these Sufis in Central Asia have brought all human being under one group. In Afghanistan, Najid fractions are other major obstacles in the path towards nationalism in Afghanistan.

The Afghan state was established in the eighteenth century, when a tribal confederation developed into a dynastic state. In 1747, Ahmad Shah Abdali led an Abdali confederation, now known as the Durrani, in the area between Persia and the Indus river. This dynasty was followed in 1818 by another Durrani dynasty, the Muhammadzai clan of the Barakzai tribe, which held power until 1978. The confederation was held together by the common aim of conquering neighbouring areas. The political and military forms of this period were characteristics of tribal warfare. War was a short-lived affair and decided upon by the council of clan chiefs of the troops or *lashkar*. The framework was that of a traditional society, but the *lashkar* usually has a supreme and temporary leader whose room for manoeuver was limited, for he was always suspected of favouring his followers. His right to lead was based upon the fact that he had been enthroned by a great tribal *Jirga* (an assembly of all the warriors). The great *Jirga* was the founding myth of the enthronement of Nadir Khan in 1929. There was no spirit of patriotism, but a profound sense of cultural identity. One's allegiance belonged to the restricted group and the tribal code (*pashtunwali*), not to the Pashtun community or to the state; to join the enemy in order the better to affirm the tribal values (vengeance or self-assertion) was not seen as constituting treachery. "To exercise Pashtu" (to identify oneself with values) was more important in the contest of the tribe than "to be a Pashtun" (to be identified with an ethnic community or a nation).[9]

The relationship between the tribal confederation and the centralized state is not to be compared with the relationship one finds in Morocco between *dar-as-siba* and *da-al-makhzam* that is to say between a tribal zone which is autonomous and a zone which is controlled by the central power. The Afghan tribes (especially the Durrani and also the Ghilzai) see the central power as their representative; it manages on their behalf the conquests that they have made together in order that the material benefits or the glory may be later shared out. The tribes see the state as existing on the periphery, responsible for administering land whose boundaries are constantly fluctuating on account of conquests carried out by the tribal confederations, in respect of which the state is no more that the means of continuity as far as their own territory is concerned. The presence of the state would seem to be redundant and totally unnecessary. The historical mission of the Afghan state may be summarized as an attempt to reverse this relationship in order to pass from the periphery to the centre. But the state could not escape the implications of the original principle, which gave it the much required legitimacy, and despite being the most Westernized one, it remained tribal and completely Pashtun.[10]

The history of he Afghan state (*dawlat*) from 1747 to the present is bound up with the search on the part of the state bureaucracy (*hukumat*) for autonomy from the tribes. The state bureaucracy has escaped the influence of tribalism in the sense that individual tribes no longer retain specific responsibilities, but it is still subject to the patronage of the clan. The development of state institutions has brought into being new social strata (intelligentsia, army, state bourgeoisie), a product of the government education system which has experienced considerable growth since 1950. These new social strata are not easily absorbed by rational society, but at the same time, they weild little influence within the state to which they owe their professional and ideological existence, for the state, as it were, the reason for their existence. In the process which has seen state bureaucracy extend to the whole of the country (both tribal and non-tribal zones), the state has made use of three modes of persuasion in order to gain legitimacy: tribalism, Islam and nationalism.[11]

When the Durrani dynasty was founded in 1747, a specific and autonomous locus ot power was established. The state that was created was a prize to be competed for in accordance with certain relatively precise rules. One clan was certain to provide the sovereign (Saddozai until 1818 and Muhammadzai until 1978). Then matrimonial alliances between families were created, from which there sprang up a complex pattern of factions intriguing against each other. This brought tribes other than the Durrani into the picture. The responsibilities of state were shared out amongst the great Durrani families (this was to remain true until 1973, at least as far as the army was concerned).There was no shortage of pretenders, who usually sprang from the immediate family (brothers and cousins), since Muslim law does not recognize the right of primogeniture. The choice was made either by consensus (the *Jirga*) or by having recourse to arms. The conflicts were often symbolic because all the pretenders were members of the Durrani, the decision was reinforced by matrimonial alliances, in which only the wives, who had come from distinguished families had any political influence. Thus an establishment came into being based upon Durrani aristocracy and the great families which had become linked with it. This establishment was cut off from its tribal origins in the sociological sense: neither the tribal code, nor the attachment to tribal zones, nor the Pashtun language retained any relevance. But the mythological reference to the tribal past which legalized their position still has a large part to play, as did the influence of groups under their patronage and genealogies. It is in this sense that one can speak of a tribal state.[12]

From the very first day right up to the present, the state has been the driving force behind modernization, providing support for new ideas and legitimizing and implementing them. Until the reign of Abdur Rehman (1880-1901), the institutions of state were indistinguishable from the court, though even by the time of Dost Mohammad (1835-63), the need for an army which was something more than a simple *lashkar* had become apparent. The reforms carried out by Abdur Rehman were not based on any reformist ideology. His conception of modernization was purely pragmatic: to rationalize the institutions of the state to make them more efficient, without thereby affecting traditional society. New techniques were adopted and key sectors were reformed, but in a piecemeal fashion. Nevertheless, this started a slow process of modernization which filtered through the body of society; but this process was a byproduct and not an end in itself. Increasing state power meant starting with the army; for that it was necessary to increase the supply of weapons and money, to create a manufacturing industry and to regionalize the fiscal system. Overnight, the state began to intervene in the economy and divide the country into neat blocks for administrative and military purposes. At the same time, the Amir, in order to curtail the influence of tribalism, for the first time focused attention upon the legal function of Islam: as the Amir, by divine right and defender of the faith, he imposed the Shariat in order to enforce state laws. He attempted to integrate the clergy with the secular institution of state by control of the *madrasa*, the *waqf*, and their wages, even going so far as to intervene in the theological domain.[13]

The introduction of these purely pragmatic reforms was carried out within the framework of the traditional exercise of power in medieval Islam. The de facto power of the Amir, who has come out on top in the contest within the tribe, was legalized by the consensus of the top in the contest within the tribe. The consensus of the tribes and the ceremony of enthronement carried out by the *Ulema*. In his turn, the Amir was charged with the responsibility of ensuring public well-being (*maslahat*) and with the task of defending religion. Within this framework, the technical reforms carried out by Abdur Rahman did not arouse any opposition. It was not just the introduction of piecemeal modernization within state institutions which was to bring society face-to face with modernity. In Afghanistan, as elsewhere, it is not modernization of some state institutions which brings problems, but modernity, the hypothesis which holds that modernization must necessarily involve a "cultural revolution", a transformation of the way of thinking and the adoption of new social paradigms.[14]

A new policy was adopted under Amanullah (1919-29). Faced with the fact that modernization had met with certain insurmountable obstacles, the state attempted to reshape and re integrate civil society. The arguments used, borrowed from the European Enlightenment and from the Salafiyya (a reformist movement) in favour of education and progress, but spiced with certain anti-clericalism, were authoritarian in nature and tended towards state control. In Afghanistan, the main lines of thought of modernist elites were laid down as early as 1911, with Tarzi in the newspaper *Seraj-ul-Akhbar* (1911-19), and were to remain unchanged by later groups including the communists, for whom the main obstacle in the way of progress was the alienation and the illiteracy of the peasants. A complete revolutionary outlook became the main condition of progress. The question of education became the recurring theme in progressive rhetoric. From 1924, the consensus between state and society, which rested largely upon a mutual indifference, was broken.[15] The result of the slow process, which resulted in the separation of the institutions of state from society, was the creation of a new political space, whose values were imposed from the West. At that time, a "tradition" came into being in response to the ever widening gulf between the people and those who held the reigns of power. In one sense, traditional society, far from existing in its own right, now became the pole of opposition to the state. Conversely, it became the shadowy projection of all the states in order to arrive at a definition of itself. The state was forced to invent a changeless, frozen world which had remained the same for centuries, incapable of coming to full consciousness of itself without "enlightenment." Here we see the significance of such metaphors as dawn, light and torch (*seraj*), which became recurrent at the end of the nineteenth century as a challenge to a seemingly obscurantist rural world. The status of the intellectual rose at the expense of the religious scholar. A good example of the views of the intelligentsia, whether liberal, Marxist or even radical Islamist, is to be found in the *Kabul Times* of 29 August 1970 (the constitutional and royalist period).

The state of the Amir of Kabul was given stability by foreign imperialism. Afghanistan became a national state because it was a buffer-state. The state was only able to impose its will upon the tribes and occupy its own territory due to the financial subsides and weapons which were freely provided by the British between 1880 and 1919. The establishment of the frontier was carried out more or less single-handedly by the British in agreement with the Russians. The British forced the Afghans to accept the Treaty of Gandarmak (May 1879) and the frontier formed by the Durand Line (1893), the Russians dictated the settlement of 1888 and 1895; all of these were underpinned by the St. Petersburg Anglo-Russian agreements of 1897. The frontiers thus defined were purely strategic and did not correspond to any ethnic or historical boundary. As an English analyst noted, "what was meant by the term scientific frontier in this connection?... it would have been impossible to demarcate on the north-west of our Indian Empire a frontier which would satisfy ethnological, political and military requirements... What was meant by a scientific frontier was the best strategic boundary which could be used as a line of defence against invasion from the direction of Central Asia."[16] There are two possible interpretations: first, a territorial and dynastic view, identified Afghanistan with the area ruled by the Amir of Kabul. The other, seeing things from a religious perspective, identified the country with the area, which had remained Muslim, surrounded as it was by the kingdoms of the infidels (Britain and Russia) or the heretics (the Persians); this was the *Millat*, the "nation" in the sense given the term in Ottoman law, that is to say a religious community. The *Millat* is a geográphical sub-region of the *umma*. This is how the great majority of the Afghan peasants have always understood the idea of the nation. Until 1924 (the date of the abolition of the Ottoman Caliphate and the first series of reforms by Amanullah), the means by which the Amir legitimized the authority of the state to rouse the people in defence of the Muslim *Millat* threatened by the infidels. But in 1924, with Afghanistan recognized by the European nations and the Caliphate abolished, such ideas became outmoded; the sate thereafter attempted a spirit of nationalism, which would be purely Afghan. The National Flag and the celebration of the National Day had already appeared during the reign of Abdur Rehman.[17] These were followed in the succeeding reigns and included a National Anthem. The constitution of 1923 defined Afghanistan as a nation in which every resident had the right of citizenship whatever his religion (no reference was made to the Muslim *Millat*). The rupture with Islamic "Indo-Aryan" past (hence the importance of archaeology), and the invention of a folklore comprising a number of incongruous elements (the National Sport was supposedly a Turkish game known as *Buzkashi*; the National Dance called *Watan*, was provincial and came from Paktia province). History was rewritten as if the political unit "Afghanistan" had existed from the earliest times. The school was, of course, the principal vehicle of this nationalist ideology.[18]

But the state always oscillated between the concepts of an abstract nation, defined on the basis of its own sovereignty, and the historical reference to a Pashtun nation defined as an ethnic group which had not yet achieved its nationhood (the only possible outcome for the other ethnic groups was to become Pashtun). While the first of these two definitions had no implications for any of the groups within the nation, the second group worked to the advantage of those Pashtuns who were not Durranis and therefore, did not belong to the tribal aristocracy. They now found an ideology in Pashtun nationalism, which gave them an opportunity to improve their social lot and the means of wresting the monopoly of power from the establishment. The group gained recruits especially amongst the young educated elite (particularly those who came from the Ghilzai), who had recently moved to the towns and were rapidly losing their tribal customs. It was amongst these that the Khalq tendency of the communist party took root, the last phase of an extreme Pashtun nationalism which, however, had only minority support, even within the linguistic community of the Pashtun. After the Soviet invasion, the resistance gathered strength and the idea of the *Millat* was revived.[19]

Afghanistan historically, culturally and geographically was a nation state. But foreign invaders have always kept Afghanistan in a state of tension and confusion. As such, historians at times have figured out Afghanistan according to their own interpretations. Afghanistan as a stable progressive independent nation state is still passing through a very critical phase. An astute leadership and political ingenuity of the present President Hamid Karzai with the help of the international community will foretell the future of Afghanistan.

REFERENCES

1. Afghan Ministry of Planning data on Afghan Agriculture, 1978, US.
2. Barnett R. Rubin. *The Fragmentation of Afghanistan: State Formation and Collapse in the International System*, New Haven, Yale University Press, 1995.
3. Beverley Male, *Revolutionary Afghanistan* (New York, St Martin's Press, 1982), p. 76.
4. Hafizullah Emadi, *Afghanistan's Gordian Knot: An Analysis of National Conflicts andStrategies for Peace*, Honolulu, East-West Centre.
5. Hafizullah Emadi, *State, Revolution and Superpowers in Afghanistan*, New York, Praeger Publishers, 1990.
6. Harvey H. Smith *et al*, (eds.), *Area Hand Book for Afghanistan*, Washington, DC: US Government Printing Office, 1973, p. 364.
7. *Ibid.*
8. *Ibid.*
9. *Ibid.*
10. *Ibid.*
11. Leon B. Poullada, *Reform and Rebellion in Afghanistan*, Ithaca and London: Cornell University Press, 1973.
12. Leonid Teplinsky, *Afghanistan: Past and Present*, Moscow: USSR Academy of Sciences, 1981.
13. Louis Dupree, *Afghanistan*, Princeton: Princeton University Press, 1973.

14. *Ibid.*
15. Roland Wild, *Amanullah, the Ex-king of Afghanistan*, London, 1932.
16. Sazinan-e-Tadaruk Bara-e-Eijadi Hizbi Kammunist Dar Afghanistan, AkhgarAfghanistan (Tehran, 1980), p. 15.
17. S. Surkha, *Afghanistan*, Kabul, Ayendagan Press, 1989.
18. Vladimir Glukhoded, *Afghanistan: Past and Present*, Moscow, USSR Academy of Science, 1981.
19. *Ibid.*

BIBLIOGRAPHY

"Afghanistan and Post-Soviet Central Asia, Prospects for Political Evolution and Islam", (United States Institute for Peace, Washington DC, 1992).

"Afghanistan", *First Consolidated Report*, Geneva, September 1988.

"Briefing by Albright and Berger on Terrorist Sites", August 22, 1998, *Wireless File* (New Delhi, 1998).

"Briefing of Donors on Afghanistan", Stockholm Donors' Meeting on Assistance for Afghanistan's Long-Term Rehabilitation and its Relationship with Humanitarian Programmes, June 1-2, 1995, p. 1.

"China's Concerns over Taliban" (Editorial), *The Frontier Post* (Peshawar, Pakistan), February 21, 2000.

"China-Iran Axis Grows in Central Asia and Afghanistan", *The Nation* (Islamabad), July 18, 2000.

"Cohen, Shelton on Anti Terrorist Strikes", August 21, 1998, *Wireless File* (New Delhi, USIS, 1998).

"Comments: Moscow's Warning to Taliban", *POT* (Afghanistan Series) (New Delhi), Vol. XXV, No. 31 (August 19, 2000).

"Data Compiled from Afghanistan Report", Institute of Strategic Studies, Islamabad (Pakistan), No. 8, November 1984.

"India is Still Without an Afghan Policy", *The Hindustan Times*, June 10, 1997.

"Iran and US Find Common Ground in Afghanistan Discussions", *International Herald Tribune*, September 18, 2000.

"Islamic Extremism – Afghan Connection", *POT* (Afghanistan Series) (New Delhi), Vol. XXV, No. 4 (February 3, 2000).

"Stability and Security a Common Concern" during Visit of General Secretary of the CPSU Central Committee, Mikhail Gorbachev to

India November 25-28, 1986, 'Documents and Materials (Moscow: Novosti Press Agency Publishing House, 1986), p. 62.

"Taliban Hang Convicted Prostitutes", *AP*, February 23, 2001.

"UNO Official Protests Taliban Interference", *The Hindu*, May 31, 2001.

"Women in Afghanistan: The Violation Continues", *Amnesty International Online*, June 1, 1997.

"Women in Afghanistan", *Factsheet* released by the Senior Coordinator for International Women's Issues, March 10, 1998, US.

"World Help Needed for Poppy Control in Afghanistan", *China Daily* (Hong Kong), February 24, 2000.

A. Banuazizi and M. Weiner, *The New Geopolitics of Central Asia and its Borderlands* (London: I. B. Tauris, 1994)

A. Doak Barnett, *Communist China and Asia: Challenge to American Policy* (New York: Vintage Looks, 1960).

A. Larmisher, *Economic Geography of Erstwhile USSR*, (Moscow, 1969).

A. Rashid, *The Resurgence of Central Asia, Islam or Nationalism?* (London: Zed Books, 1994)

A. Rasul, A., *Afghanistan Through A Critical Phase of History*, (Peshawar, 1996).

A. S. Ahmad, "Tribe and States in Waziristan", In Richard Tapper (ed.), *The Conflict of Tribe and State in Iran and Afghanistan* (London, 1983), pp. 192-211.

A. S. Giridharadas, *Afghanistan and 9/11* (Rolie Books, New Delhi, 2002).

Abdul Samad Ghaus, *The Fall of Afghanistan: An Insider's Account* (Washington and New York: Pergamon-Brassey's, 1988), p. 89.

Abha Dixit, "Taliban, Pakistan and India's Afghan Policy", *The Pioneer*, June 3, 1997.

Afghanistan Report, Nos. 22-37, 1989.

Afghanistan Series (New Delhi), Vol. XXV, No. 29, August 5, 2000.

Afghanistan, *Democratic Republic of Afghanistan's Annual, 1979* (Kabul: Government Printing House, 1979), pp. 81-89.

Afghanistan, *Strategic Studies* (Islamabad), Spring 2002.

Afghanistan: Crisis of Impunity: The Role of Pakistan, Russia and Iran in Fueling the Civil War, Human Rights Watch July 2001, pp. 27-28.

Agence France-Press, December 2, 1999.

Ahmad Rashid, "Afghanistan: Taliban Temptation", *Far Eastern Economic Review* (Hong Kong), March 11, 1999.

Ahmad Rashid, "Divisions Multiply", *Far Eastern Economic Review*, July 1997, p. 21.

Ahmad Rashid, *Taliban: Militant Islam, Oil and Fundamentalism in Central Asia* (Yale University Press, 2001).

Ahmad Rashid, *The Resurgence of Central Asia: Islam or Nationalism?* (Oxford University Press, 1994).

Ahmed Rashid, "Afghanistan: Heart of Darkness", *Far Eastern Economic Review* (Hong Kong), August 5, 1999, p. 11.

Ahmed Rashid, "Back with a Vengeance: Proxy War in Afghanistan", *The World Today*, Vol. 52, No. 3, March 1996.

Ahmed Rashid, "The Chinese Connection", *The Herald*, Karachi, Pakistan, Vol. 26, No.12 (December 1995).

Ahmed Rashid, "The Taliban: Exporting Extremism", *Foreign Affairs*, Vol. 78, No. 6, November/December 1999, p. 35.

Ahsan Ali Khan, "Is There a Method in Afghan Raids?" *The Muslim*, March 20, 1987.

Akbar S. Ahmad, *Pakhtun Economy and Society*, London, 1980, pp. 181, 193.

Ali K. Ahmad, *Frontier Discord between Afghanistan and Pakistan*, March 1951.

Ali Wardak, "The Ethnic and Tribal Composition of Afghan Society", In Girardet and Walter (eds.), *Afghanistan: Essential Field Guides to Humanitarian and Conflict Zone* (Geneva, 1998), pp. 85-86.

Ali, S. Iqbal, *Modern Afghanistan* (London, 1938).

Amera Saeed, "Afghanistan: Peshawar Accord and After", *Regional Studies*, Spring 1993, pp. 103-158.

Amin Saikal and William Maley, *Regime Change in Afghanistan: Foreign Intervention and the Politics of Legitimacy* (Boulder: Westview Press, 1991).

Amstutz, *Afghanistan*, published by *Strategic Studies*, Islamabad, 1984.

Amstutz, *Afghanistan*, US and UK, 1986.

Amstutz, *Russia's War in Afghanistan*, London, 1986.

Amustutz, *Afghanistan and the Soviet Union*, 1985, p. 101.

Andrey Gillan, "Pakistani Hit Squad was Trained by the CIA to Kill Bin Laden", *Guardian*, October 4, 2001.

Ann Marlowe, "Warlords and Leaders", *National Review Online*, February 18, 2002.

Annual Report 1990-91, Ministry of External Affairs, External Publicity Division, Government of India, New Delhi, 1991.

Annual Report, 1999-2000, Ministry of External Affairs, External Publicity Division, Government of India, New Delhi, 2000.

Anthony Arnold, *Afghanistan: The Soviet Invasion in Perspective*, (Stanford: Hoover Institution Press), 1985.

Anthony Davis, "Anguish Continues in Afghanistan", *Jane's Intelligence Review*, Vol. 8, No. 12, December 1996.

Anthony Davis, "Xinjiang learns to Live with Resurgent Islam", *Jane's Intelligence Review*, September 1996.

Anthony Davis, *How the Taliban Became a Military Power, Fundamentalism Reborn*? (New York: New York University Press, 1997)

Anthony Hyman "Central Asia's Relations with Afghanistan in South Asia", in *The New Central Asia and its Neighbours*, (London, 1994), pp. 76-78.

Anthony Hyman, *Russia, Central Asia and the Taliban*, New Delhi.

Asian Survey (Berkeley), Vol. 38, No. 2, February 1998, p. 115.

Assem Akram, *Afghan Communism and Soviet Intervention*, (Oxford University Press, 1999).

Associated Press, April 10, 2000.

B. A. Islamov, *Post-Soviet Central Asia and the CIS: The Economic background of Interdependence* (Oxford, 1994).

Barnett, R. Rubin, "Afghanistan under the Taliban", *Current History* (Philadelphia), Vol. 98, No. 625, February 1999, p. 90.

Barnett R. Rubin, "The Fragmentation of Afghanistan", *Foreign Affairs*, Vol. 68, No. 5 (Winter 1989-90).

Barnett R. Rubin, *The Fragmentation of Afghanistan: State Formation and Collapse in the International System* (New Haven: Yale University Press, 1995).

Barnett R. Rubin, *The Search for Peace in Afghanistan: From Buffer State to Failed State* (New Haven: Yale University Press, 1995).

Barton Gellman and Thomas Ricks, "US Concludes Bin Laden escaped at Tora Bora Fight", *The Washington Post*, p. Al, April 17, 2002.

Beatrice Forbes Manz, *Central Asia Historical Background* (New York, 1994).

Beatrice Forbes Manz, *The Rise and Rule of Tamerlane*, (Cambridge: Cambridge University Press, 1989).

Bess Brown, "Die Angst Zentralasiens vor dem russischen Baren", *Interlaminate Politic*, Vol. 50, No. 11, November 1995, pp. 51-56.

Bess Brown, "Three Central Asian states from Economic Union", *RFE/RL Research Report*, Vol. 3, No.13. April 1, 1994.

Beverley Male, *Revolutionary Afghanistan*, (New York: St Martin's Press, 1982).

Boris Rumer, "The potential for Political Instability and Regional Conflicts", in *The New Geopolitics of Central Asia and its Borderlands* (Londres, London, I. B. Tauris, 1994).

Bradsher, *Afghanistan and the Soviet Union* (London, 1985).

Brigadier A. R. Siddiqi, "Dealing with Taliban", *The Nation* (Islamabad), July 12, 2000.

C. Raja Mohan, "US Sanctions Against Taliban Seen Endorsing Indian Stand on Terrorism", *The Hindu* (New Delhi, December 21, 2000.

Central Asia Monitor, No. 1, 1994, US.

Central Asian Survey, Vol. 13, No. 1, 1994 (London).

Central Intelligence Agency World Facts on Afghanistan, 2001.

Charles M. Macgregor, *Central Asia Part 6* (Foreign Department Press, 1873).

Cheryl Bernard on National Public Radio's "Fresh Air Programme", April 17, 2002.

Clinton's Oval Office Remarks on Anti Terrorist Attacks, August 21, 1998, Office Text (New Delhi, 1998).

David Cotright and George A. Lopez, *The Sanctions Decade: Assessing UN Strategies in the 1990s*.

Dennis Kux, *The United States and Pakistan, 1947-2000*, (Johns Hopkins, 2000), p. 245.

Diego Cordovez and Selig S. Harrison, *Out of Afghanistan: The Inside Story of the Soviet Withdrawal*, (New York: Oxford University Press, 1995).

Dileep Mukerji, "Case for Indian Neutrality", March 2, 1988.

Donald N. Wilber, *Afghanistan* (London and New York, 1956).

Donald, N. Wilber, *Afghanistan, Its People, Its Society* (London, 1989).

Douglas A. *Bore, Superpowers Defeated: Vietnam and Afghanistan Compared* (London: Frank Cass, 1999).

Dr. Babar Shah, *Geo-Strategic Patterns of a Post-Taliban* (US, 1990).

Dr. Zbigniew Brzezinski in an interview with Le Nouvel Observatory, January 14, 1998.

E. Shevardnadze, *The Future Belongs to Freedom* (New York, 1991).

E. T. Dugdab, *German Diplomatic Documents* (New York, 1960).

E. Theodore, "Afghanistan in 1990", *Asian Survey*, Vol. 31, No. 2, February 1991.

Edward Girardet, *Afghanistan: The Soviet War* (London: Helm, 1988).

Elizabeth E. Bacon *Central Asians under Russian Rule: A Study in Cultural Change* (Cornell University, 1966).

Excerpts from the Memoirs of Zeki Velidi Togan, H. B. Paksoy (ed.), *The Rediscovery of History* (New York: M. E. Sharpe, 1994).

Facts on File, March 25, 1999, p. 208.

Facts on File, New York, April 23, 1992, pp. 285-86.

Facts on File, September 5, 1996, p. 650.

Fannina W. Halle, *Women in the Soviet East* (New York, 1938).

Fazal-ur-Rehman, "Pakistan's Relations with China", *Strategic Studies* (Islamabad), Vols. XIX and Xx, Nos. 1 and 4, Winter/Spring 1998.

Free Afghanistan Report, February 1990.

Free Afghanistan Report, Special Edition, January/February 1988.

Frontier Post, November 1, 2000.

G. Kish, *Economic Atlas of Soviet Union* (US, 1960).

Geoffrey Wheeler, *The Modern History of Soviet Central Asia* (London, Weidenfeld and Nicholson, 1964).

George Arney, *Afghanistan: Definitive Account of a Country at Crossroad* (Mandarin, 1990). It is now out of Press.

Gilles Dorronsoro, *War, Politics and Society in Afghanistan: 1978-1992* (London, 1978).

Girilal Jain, "An Indian Afghan Policy: No Need to Get Involved", *Times of India*, March 2, 1988.

Guenter Lewy, *America in Vietnam* (New York: Oxford University, Press, 1978).

H. W. Bellew, *A Dictionary of the Pukkhto or Pushkto Languages* (Lahore, 1901).

Hafizullah Emadi, *Politics of Development and Women in Afghanistan* (New York: Paragon House Publishers, 1993).

Hafizullah Emadi, *State, Revolution and Superpowers in Afghanistan* (New York: Praeger, 1990).

Harvey W. Nelson, *Power and Security: Beijing, Moscow and Washington* (London, 1989).

Henry Lansdell, *Through Central Asia* (London, 1887).

Henry S. Bradsher, *Afghanistan and the Soviet Union* (Durham: Duke University Press, 1985).

Herbert Dieter, *Regional Integration in Zentralasien*, US, 1996.

I. K. Gujral, "A Foreign Policy for India", External Publicity Division, Ministry of External Affairs, Government of India, New Delhi, 1998.

Ilyas Khan, "The ISI-Taliban Nexus", *Herald*, November 2001, p. 26.

IMF Report on Erstwhile Russian Economic Federation, US, 1993.

IMF Report on World Bank Organization for Economic Co-operation and Development: A Study of Erstwhile Soviet Economies, US, 2000.

Indian Express, February 20, 2000.

International Herald Tribune, September, 22, 2000.

Intikhab Amir, "Wooing the West?" *The Herald*, March 1999, pp. 60a-60b.

James M. Scott, *Deciding to Intervene: The Reagan Doctrine and American Foreign Policy* (Durham: Duke University Press, 1996).

Jan Goodwin, " An Uneasy Peace", *The Nation*, April 29, 2002.

Jerry F. Hough, *The Struggle for the Third World: Soviet Debates and American Options* (Washington DC: The Brookings Institution, 1986).

Joan Rosita Forbes, *Forbidden Road: Kabul to Samarkand* (London: Cassell, 1937).

John Donnelly and Anthony Shadid, "US Talking with Afghan Opposition", *The Boston Globe*, September 18, 2001.

John F. Burns and Steve Levine, "For Afghans, Taliban's Rise to Power Was Deliverance from Tyranny", *International Herald Tribune*, January 2, 1997.

John F. Burns, "New Afghan Force Takes Hold, Turning to Peace", *New York Times*, p. A3, February 16, 1995.

John K. Cooley, *Unholy Wars: Afghanistan, America and International Terrorism* (London: Pluto Press, 1999).

John L. S. Girling, *America and the Third World: Revolution and Intervention* (London: Routledge & Keegan Paul, 1980).

Jon W. Anderson and Richard F. Strand (eds.), "Ethnic Processes and Inter-group Relations in Contemporary Afghanistan", *Occasional Paper No.15*, Afghan Council of the Asia Society (Summer 1978).

Joshua Kunitz, *Dawn Over Samarkand* (New York, 1935).

Julie Sirrs, "The Taliban's Foreign Righter, Committee for a Free Afghanistan, November 11, 2000.

K. B. Harpviken, "Transcending Traditionalism: The Emergence of Non State Military Formations in Afghanistan", *Journal of Peace Research*, Vol. 34, No. 3, 1997, pp. 271-87.

K. Gharabaghi, "Development Strategies for Central Asia in the 1990s: In Search of Alternatives", *Third World Quarterly*, Vol. 15, No. 1, 1994.

K. Robert, " Afghanistan Postmortem", *The Atlantic*, April 1989, p. 26.

Kamal Matinuddin, *Pakistan's Policy Towards Afghanistan and Central Asia* (University of Peshawar, Pakistan, 2000).

Kathy Gannon, "Taliban Warns US Against Curbs," *Times of India*, November 10, 1999.

Khalid Mahmud, "China Revisited Part II: Old Friends Learning New Ways", *The News* (Islamabad), June 21, 1998.

Kissing's Record of World Events (London), Vol. 45, No.7/8, July 1999, p. 43064.

L. Steve, "Hidden Hand", *Newsweek*, October 17, 1997.

Leon B. Poullada, *Reform and Rebellion in Afghanistan: King Amanullah's Failure to Modernize a Tribal Society* (Ithaca and London: Cornell University Press, 1919-29).

Lillian Craig Harris, "Xinjiang, Central Asia and the Implications for China's Policy in the Islamic World", *The China Quarterly*, London, No. 133, March 1993.

Louis Dupree, *Afghanistan* (Princeton: Princeton University Press, 1980).

Louis Dupree, *Post-withdrawal Afghanistan* (Great Britain, 1989).

Louis Dupree, *Soviet Intervention in Afghanistan*, Paper delivered at the 1989, Annual Meeting of the American Political Science Association, New Orleans, 1985.

Louis Dupree, *The Soviet Withdrawal from Afghanistan* (UK, 1992).

M. Ehsan Ahrari, "The Dynamics of the New Great Game in Central Asia", *Central Asian Survey*, Vol. 13, No. 4, 1994.

M. Ehsan Ehrari, "China, Pakistan and the Taliban Syndrome", *Asian Survey* (California), Vol. XL, No. 4, July/August, 2000.

M. Richard, "Afghan People Never Say Die", Insight, January 25, 1988.

M. Sliwinski "On the Routes of 'Hijrat", *Central Asian Survey*, Vol. 8, No. 4, 1989, pp. 69-93.

M. Spencer, "A Message from the Executive Director", *Free Afghanistan Report*, February 1990.

Mardin, *Civil Society and Islam in Civil Society* (Cambridge: Polity Press, 1995).

Marin Strmecki, "Winning Truly in Afghanistan", *National Review Online*, May 20, 2002.

Mark Urban, *War in Afghanistan* (London: Macmillan, 1990).

Martin McCauley, *Agriculture in Central Asia and Kazakhstan in the 1980s*, 1994.

Marvin Weinbaum, *Pakistan and Afghanistan: Resistance and Reconstruction* (Lahore Book Corporation, 1994).

Michael Griffin, *Reaping the Whirlwind: The Taliban Movement in Afghanistan* (London: Pluto Press, 2001).

Milan Hauner and Robert L. Canfield (eds.), *Afghanistan and the Soviet Union: Collision and Transformation* (Boulder, Westview Press, 1989).

Mohammad Yousuf and Mark Adkin, The Bear Trap (Lahore, Jang Publishers, 1992).

Mujtaba Razvi, *The Frontiers of Pakistan: A Study of Frontier Problems in Pakistan's Foreign Policy* (Karachi, Dacca: National Publishing House 1971).

N. A. Khalidi, *Demographic Profile of Afghanistan* (The Australian National University, Canberra, 1989).

N. Newill, *The Struggle for Afghanistan* (UK, 1991).

N. Shahrani, "Central Asia and the Challenge to Soviet legacy", *Central Asian Survey*, Vol. 12, No. 2, 1993.

N. Sharrani, "Central Asia and the Challenge of Soviet legacy", *Central Asian Survey*, Vol. 12, No. 2, 1993.

Nancy Hatch Dupree, "Afghan Women Under The Taliban", William Maley (ed.), *Fundamentalism Reborn? Afghanistan and The Taliban* (London: Hurst and Company, 1988).

Nancy Hatch Dupree, *Afghan Women under the Taliban, Fundamentalism Reborn*? (New York, New York University Press, 1997).

Naveed Ahmad Tahir, "Pakistan's Afghan Policy: The Regional and International Dimensions", *Pakistan* Horizon, Karachi, Vol. 53, No.1, January 2000.

New York Times, September 11, 1997.

Novosti, Dushanbe, September 19, 2000.

Novosti, Moscow, September 26, 2000.

Olivier Roy, *Islam and Resistance in Afghanistan* (Cambridge: Cambridge University Press, 1985).

Owens Lattimore, *Studies in Frontier History* (London, 1962).

P. E. Lydolph, *Geography of USSR* (Wills, 1977).

P. J. Taylor, *Political Geography, World-Economy, Nation-State and Locality* (Longman, 1991).

P. Stobdan, "China's Central Asian Dilemma", *Strategic Analysis*, New Delhi, Vol. XXII, No. 3, June 1999.

P. Stobdan, "The Afghan Conflict and India", *Delhi Paper 6*, Institute of Defence Studies and Analyses, New Delhi, 1998.

P. Stobdan, "The Afghan Conflict and Regional Security", *Strategic Analysis* (New Delhi), Vol. 23, No. 5, August 1999.

Peter W. Rodman, *More Precious than Peace: The Cold War and the Struggle for the Third World* (New York, Scribner's, 1994).

Q. Reshliya, *Rivers of Afghanistan* (Afghanistan, April 1947).

R. Hager, "State, Tribe and Empire in Afghan Inter-Polity Relations", in Richard Tapper (ed.), *The Conflict of Tribe and State in Iran and Afghanistan* (London, 1983).

R. Hutchins, *Soviet Economic Development* (Oxford, 1978).

R. Israeli, "Return to the Source: the Republics of Central Asia and the Middle East, *Central Asia Survey*, Vol. 13, No. 1, 1994.

R. Millor, *Erstwhile Soviet Union and its Geographical Problems* (London, 1982).

Ralph. H. Magnus, "Afghanistan in 1996-Year of the Taliban", *Asian Survey*, Vol. 37, No. 2, February, 1997, p. 111.

Rape and B. Naslee, *Women in the Transition to Socialism* (New York, 1989).

Rasul Baksh Rais, "Afghanistan after Soviet Withdrawal", *Asian Survey*, Vol. 91, No. 563, March 1992, p.125.

Redek Sikorski "Afghanistan Revisited", *National Review*, August 23, 1993, pp. 40-42.

Report by L. Canfield, "Ethnic, Regional and Sectarian Alignments in Afghanistan" in *The State, Religion and Ethnic Politics: Pakistan, Iran and Afghanistan* (Islamabad, University Press, 1986).

Report in UN Chronicle, New York, Vol. 35, No.4, October-December, 1998, p. 58.

Report of the Secretary General on the Situation of Women and Girls in Afghanistan, Economic and Social Council, United Nations, July 21, 2000.

Report of the Secretary-General on Emergency Assistance to Afghanistan in Doc. A/52/536, 28 October 1997, Para 11.

Report of the UN Secretary-General, "The Situation in Afghanistan and its Implications for International Peace and Security" (New York: United Nations, 1999).

Revolutions and Rebellions in Afghanistan (Institute of Intermission Studies, University of California, Berkeley, 1984).

Riaz M. Khan, *Untying the Afghan Knot: Negotiating Soviet Withdrawal* (Durham: Duke University Press, 1991).

Rizwan Qureshi, "The Afghan War Visits Peshawar", *The Herald,* March 1999, pp.62-64.

Robert Gurr, "Ethnic Warfare on the Wane", *Foreign Affairs,* Vol. 79, No. 3, May-June 2000, pp. 52-64.

Robert L. Canfield, "Hazara Integration into the Afghan Nation: Some Changing Relations between Hazaras and Afghan Officials", *Occasional Paper No.3,* The Afghan Council, New York, 1972, p.6.

Roland Gotz, 'Die Wirtschaft der Mitglieder der Gmeeinschaft unabhangiger Staaten (GUS), Teil III: Die Zentralasiatischen Staaten "Kazakhstan, Kirgistan. Tadschikistan. Turkmenistan und Uzbekistan", BIOST: Aktuelle Analyses, No.31, US, 1995.

Roland Wild, *Ammanullah: Ex-King of Afghanistan* (London, 1932).

Roland, Dannreuther, "Russia, Central Asia and the Persian Gulf", *The IISS Quarterly,* December 1994, pp. 92-112.

S. Goldenberg, *Pride of Small Nations. The Caucasus and Post-Soviet Disorder* (London, 1994).

S. M. Y., *Sovietization of Afghanistan* (Peshawar, 1986).

S. Nasir, *Soviet Expansion in the Third World: Afghanistan: A Case Study* (Bartleby Press, 1986).

S. Niel MacFarlane, "Humanitarian Action and Conflict", *International Journal,* Ottawa, Vol. 54, No. 4, Autumn 1999, p. 542.

S. Radek, "Afghanistan Revised", *National Review,* August 23, 1993, pp. 40-42.

S.N. Richard, *The Struggle for Afghanistan* (University Press, 1981).

Saeed Hasan, "Living in a New Neighbourhood", *The News,* (Islamabad), March 3, 1998.

Salamat Ali, "A Peace on Paper", *Far Eastern Economic Review,* March 18, 1993, p. 22.

Sardar Ikbal Ali Shah, *Afghanistan of the Afghans* (New Delhi: Bhavana Books & Prints), First Reprint 2000.

Sazmain-e-Tadaruk Bara-e-Eijadi Hizbi Kamunist Dar Afghanistan (Akhgar), Afghanistan (Tehran: n.p., 1980).

Security Council Resolution 1214 of December 8, 1997.

Security Council Resolution 1333 of 19 December, 2000.

Seminar on NGOs and Civil Society (Tashkent: UNDP, 1994).

Seth Mydans, "Pakistan's Hard Line on Terror Shows Signs of Softening", *The New York Times,* April 28, 2002.

Seymour Hersh, "Annals of National Security: The Gateway", *The New Yorker (The New York Times)*, January 28, 2002, pp. 36037.

Sharad K. Soni, "The United National Commission on Human Rights, 55th Session, March-April, 1999: A Report", *Himalayan and Central Asian Studies*, New Delhi, Vol. 4, No.2, April-June 2000, p. 47.

Sheila Marnie and Whitlock, "Central Asia and Economic Integration", *RFE/RL Research Report*, Vol. 2, No. 14, April 2, 1993, pp. 34-44.

Shirin Tahirkheli, *The United States and Pakistan: The Evolution of an Influence Relationship* (New York: Praeger Publishers, 1982).

Speech by S. K. Lamba, India's Special Envoy on Afghanistan, at the India International Centre, New Delhi, on February 11, 2002.

Sreedhar and Mahendra Ved, *Afghan: Power Games and Gamesmen*, Vol. 1 (Delhi: Worth Smith, 2000).

Statistical Indicators for Asia and Pacific (US, 1994-2000).

Sultan Mohammad Khan, "Responding to New Realities", *Dawn* (Karachi), August 7, 2000.

Surya Gangadharan, "The China-Taliban Equation", *Aakrosh* (New Delhi), Vol. 3, No. 6, January 2000.

Swaran Singh, "India and the Shanghai Forum", *Strategic Analysis*, New Delhi, Vol. XXIV, No. 5, September 2000.

T. Ragers, *The Soviet Withdrawal Rom Afghanistan* (New York, 1992).

Ted Mataxis, *Free Afghanistan Report*, February 1990, p. 3.

The Hindu, April 1, 1998.

The Hindu, August 30, 1990.

The Hindu, December 21, 2000.

The Hindu, December 27, 1987.

The Hindu, February 14, 1988.

The Hindu, January 13, 1988.

The Hindu, March 24, 1997.

The Hindu, November 24, 1999.

The Hindu, November 3, 1999.

The Hindu, October 10, 1999.

The Hindu, October 27, 1999.

The Hindustan Times, April 18, 1996.

The Hindustan Times, March 31, 1989.

The Hindustan Times, October 26, 1999.

The New York Times, April 10, 1998.

The New York Times, April 18, 1998.

The New York Times, April 21, 1998.

The New York Times, April 27, 1998.

The New York Times, September 15, 1998.

The Pioneer (New Delhi), May 27, 1997.

The Telegraph (Calcutta), August 26, 1998.

The Telegraph (Kolkata), March 17, 1999

The Times of India, December 25, 1987.

The Times of India, January 18, 1988.

The Times of India, May 4, 1988.

The Tribune (Chandigarh), December 31, 1999.

The Tribune, (Chandigarh), January 6, 2000.

The Tribune, (Chandigarh), October 16, 1996.

The Year Book of the United Nations, 1996.

Thomas J. Barfield, "The Impact of Pashtun Immigration on Nomadic Pastoralism in Northeastern Afghanistan."

Thomas T. Hammond, *Red Flag over Afghanistan: The Communist Coup, the Soviet Invasion, and the Consequences* (Boulder, Westview Press, 1984).

UN Newsletter, Vol. 51, No. 42, October 19, 1996.

UN Newsletter, Vol. 54, No. 44, November 6, 1999.

UN Newsletter, Vol. 54, No. 46, November 20, 1999.

UN Newsletter, Vol. 55, No. 14, April 1, 2000.

UN Newsletter, Vol. 55, No. 33, August 12, 2000.

UN Newsletter, Vol. 55, No. 42, October 14, 2000.

UN Newsletter, Vol. 55, No. 48, 25 November 2000.

UN Newsletter, Vol. 55, No. 9, 26 February 2000.

UNI Report from Moscow, November 4, 2000.

United Nations: The Geneva Accords–Agreements on the Settlement of the Situation Relating to Afghanistan (New York Department of Public Information, July 1988).

US Committee for Refugees, *World Refugee Survey* (Washington, DC: American Council for Nationalities Service, 1989).

US State Department's *Human Rights Report for Afghanistan*, 1999, pp. 19-20.

V. Gregorian, *Emergence of Modern Afghanistan* (California, 1969).

Vatan Gregorian, *The Emergence of Modern Afghanistan* (California, 1969).

Vladimir Glukhoded, *Afghanistan: Past and Present* (Moscow: USSR Academy of Science, 1981).

Vyacheslav Belokrenitsky, "Russian-Afghan Relations", (London, Oxford University Press, 1999).

W. Fred Starr and Marin Strmecki, "Time to Ditch the Northern Alliance", *The Wall Street Journal*, February 28, 2002.

W. Maley, *United Nations and Afghanistan* (New York University Press, New York).

Wendy Zea Goldman, *Women, the Family and the New Revolutionary Order in the Soviet Union* (US, 1989).

William L. Shirer, *The Rise and Fall of the Third Reich* (London, Pan Books, 1964).

William Maley, *Afghanistan and the Taliban* (US, 1990).

William Maley, *Reconstructing Afghanistan* (London, 1999).

William Maley, *The Soviet Withdrawal from Afghanistan* (Cambridge: Cambridge University Press, 1989).

William Maley, *The UN in Afghanistan: Doing its best or Failure of a Mission*, London, 1998.

William Maley, *The United Nations and Afghanistan, Fundamentalism Reborn?* (London and New York, New York University Press, 1997).

World Bank World Development Report (Washington, Oxford University Press, 1995).

World Fact Book Afghanistan Section (UK, 1993).

World Trade Organization Report (Geneva, 1995).

Zalmay Khalilzad, "Afghanistan in 1995: Civil War and Mini Great Game", *Asian Survey*, Vol. 36, No. 2, February 1996, p. 195.

Zalmay Khalilzad, *Afghanistan: Consolidation of a Rogue State* (US, 2000).

Index